Imagine the Possibilities

YOUR TIME IS NOW

Cindy Heil

Destiny
ALIGNMENT
Coaching Consulting Art Design

edited and expanded

All scripture quotations, unless otherwise noted, are taken from the New American Standard Bible ©1960, 1962, 1963, 1968, 1971, 1972, 1975, 1977 The Lockman Foundation

Imagine the Possibilities - Your Time is Now
Edited and Expanded

ISBN-13: 978-0983977919
ISBN-10: 0983977917

Copyright © 2011, 2017 by Cindy Heil

Published by Destiny Alignment
www.DestinyAlignment.com

Cover Design by Cindy Heil

Printed in the United States of America

Images courtesy of NASA

ACKNOWLEDGEMENTS

To all those who listened patiently

while I thought out loud and bounced

ideas off you, who gave your thoughts,

suggestions, and corrections,

I thank you.

Your teamwork made an enjoyable

journey even more fun.

DEDICATION

TO MY LORD JESUS CHRIST – You take all I give you and You turn it into treasure. You patiently teach me and patiently wait until I get it. You never give up on me. You open my eyes to see beyond where I am today, and show me more beauty than I ever thought possible. Every day with You is more exciting than the day before.

TO MY PARENTS – You have always given your love, your support and your encouragement, and you believe in me to be able to reach as high as I can reach and go as far as I can go. You always love me right where I am.

TO MY SISTERS – It is a blessing to have such wonderful sisters who are also great friends. Thank you for always being there.

TABLE OF CONTENTS

Thus says the Lord, "Stand by the ways and see and ask for the ancient paths, where the good way is, and walk in it; And you shall find rest for your souls."

Jeremiah 6:16

Come to Me, all you who are weary and heavy laden, and I will give you rest. Take My yoke upon you, and learn from Me, for I am gentle and humble in heart; and you shall find rest for your souls. For My yoke is easy, and My load is light.

Matthew 11:28-30

FOREWORD

This book is written to be an "easy read." I don't want you to have to work to get through it. It is my desire that you sit back, relax, grab a cup of coffee, and let God speak to you as you read.

There was a season when I was seeking the Lord about doing the works that He did and how to see more of that in my life, and I asked Him to help me teach other believers whatever He showed me. His answer was, "Your traditions are making My Word of no effect." (Mark 7:7, 8,9,13, Matthew 15:6) So from then on I gave Him permission to reveal those traditions so I could get rid of them, and to show me His truth, confirming all with the testimony of 2 or 3 scriptures. (He always led me to way more than 3.) I was surprised at the things He showed me in the days and years that followed. There were many things I had *believed because I had always been taught them, but when He showed me what the Word had to say, I realized that I was believing wrong about those things. They looked good, sounded good, made me look good, they were what "everyone" was teaching and believing, but, if they were making God's Word of no effect in my life, they were way too expensive and I wanted them gone. Some of the things discussed in this book may challenge you to look at things and think about things differently than you have been. Ask God to help you understand His truth and to show you new things He wants to reveal to you.*

"Imagine the Possibilities" is not intended as an in-depth study of the information contained in these pages. There is much more that can be said about the subjects discussed here. I offer this manuscript as an introduction – an introduction to the greatness of God, an introduction to the greatness of all He created you to be, and an introduction to all the

possibilities that await you in Him. In Jesus the veil has been lifted and we can see past the now and into what God has reserved for us. And we have a great hope – a confident expectation of good. The God of Heaven and Earth is the God of hope and a life with Him is all about hope.

When we were without God, we had no hope.

"Remember that you were at that time separate from Christ, excluded from the commonwealth of Israel, and strangers to the covenants of promise, having no hope and without God in the world."   *Eph 2:12*

But now, because of what Jesus has done for us, we can abound in hope because He is the God of hope.

"Now may the God of hope fill you with all joy and peace in believing, so that you will abound in hope by the power of the Holy Spirit."

Romans 15:13

And because of how much He loves us that hope does not disappoint.

"And hope does not disappoint, because the love of God has been poured out within our hearts through the Holy Spirit Who was given to us." Romans 5:5

Your hopes and your dreams may have been buried or you may have long since given up on them. You may have become afraid to dream, afraid to hope. But be encouraged. What awaits you is a whole new beginning. With Jesus, it's not about your past, it's about your future. And with God, nothing is impossible – because the cross changed everything.

Relax.

Enjoy.

Receive.

Cindy

Founder and President, Destiny Alignment

When you hook up with God it is impossible for anything to be impossible

INTRODUCTION

PERHAPS ONE OF THE MOST MEMORABLE quotes from the movie "Apollo 13," whether it really happened in the midst of the Houston control center or it was just a line in a script, is the heart of this book. *"Failure is not an option."* It is what God says concerning you. In His eyes you are a complete success.

Already.

Right now.

Because He sees you as He created you to be.

God created you for success and designed you for dominion.

His plans for you are for total victory. He has never once looked at you and said,

"Ooops!" When your loving heavenly Father looks at you, He doesn't see a failure or a disappointment. He sees the apple of His Eye, His cherished child. He sees in you all the potential He placed in you from the foundation of the world.

> *If you could see yourself as God sees you, you wouldn't recognize yourself!*

You see, you are not a surprise to God. He knew about you all along. He knows all your strengths and all your weaknesses, and He went to great lengths to plan for you, to prepare for you, make a way for you, and provide for you.[1] If you could see yourself as God sees you, you wouldn't recognize yourself! You are so much more beautiful, so much more gifted and talented than you've probably ever given yourself credit for. You are created in His image – you've been created to act like Him. And you are created in His likeness – you've been created to look like Him.[2] The word "image" means shadow. A shadow moves exactly like the one casting that shadow. The word "likeness" means appearance. So you were created to move exactly like God and to look like Him!

Often we don't see ourselves as we really are because we aren't looking in the right direction. We have been comparing ourselves to others, to the latest Hollywood idol, or to our own self-made, self-developed ideals. But you weren't created in Hollywood's image. You weren't created to be like someone else, nor was anyone else created to be like you. You were created to look like and act like God Himself, to possess the beauty of the kingdom of God!

Imagine being beautiful by Heaven's standard of beauty – by perfection's standard of beauty. Imagine being treasured and valued by the very kingdom of God – by the angels and by God Himself!

Well – you are!

You are a valued, treasured citizen of the kingdom of God, and all of Heaven is here to defend you, protect you. He has given His angels charge concerning you – to bear you up in their hands![3]

You're the King's kid!

You were created by the Creator of the universe, not as an insignificant piece of flesh that was deposited in the earth and forgotten, but as a vibrant, vital and valuable part of His plan and His kingdom.

You have His attributes and His characteristics, and He is building His character in you. He has a plan for you, a future for you, and a destiny for you.[4]

He is smiling over you.

He is rejoicing over you.[5]

He is laughing with pleasure and joy over who you are now and over all you are going to become and do.

> *No one can be you as good as you can*

Your combination of gifts, talents, and passions is completely unique. No one else before you, and no one else after you, has ever had or will ever have that exact same combination. You are a one–of–a–kind.

You are intentionally unique. No one can be you as good as you can. No one else can be the you that you were created to be.

Now is the time to turn your eyes from the lesser to the greater, from Hollywood to the Kingdom, and begin to see yourself as you really are.

The A, B, Cs of Destiny Alignment are –

It's never too late to **A**CHIEVE

It's never too late to **B**ECOME

It's never too late to **C**HANGE

BECAUSE THE CROSS CHANGED

EVERYTHING!

It's your turn.

It's your time.

*To have faith simply means to
agree with God*

CHAPTER ONE

APOLLO 13

NASA'S SUCCESSFUL FAILURE

I HAVE ALWAYS HAD A SPECIAL PLACE in my heart for the space program. My dad worked with the space program – Mercury, Gemini, Titan, Apollo, Skylab – so I grew up with it in a special way. I have a great admiration for all those men and women who collectively did what had never been done before. It took courage, trust, teamwork, and never being satisfied with yesterday's achievements to press on to what was next.

There were massive victories and heartbreaking defeats, but through it all they persevered. They have given us a legacy and a future that would not have been possible otherwise.

25

The Apollo 13 mission was particularly spectacular. It has been called NASA's successful failure. It is also called NASA's finest hour. They did not achieve what they set out to do, yet they accomplished so much more than they ever thought possible.

> *They couldn't be sure it would work,*
> *but it was all they had*

Their mission was to land on the moon, but early on in the flight they experienced an explosion that rendered the service module nonfunctional. It was a devastating, mission crippling problem that cost them the moon and threatened to cost them their lives. The ship that was designed to provide them oxygen, water and power and to maneuver them home – Odyssey – was damaged beyond repair and could no longer be used for the functions for which it was originally designed. The only ship they could now use – Aquarius – was designed only for landing on the moon. But because of the damage to Odyssey, it was the only option they had to perform the maneuvers necessary to get them safely back to Earth. They couldn't be sure it would work. But it was all they had.

They booted up Aquarius and shut down Odyssey.

The Lunar module was not designed to do what it was now being asked to do. It had never been tested under these conditions. If the crew was to return safely, failure was not an option. Together with the flight crew, those on the ground had to come up with the way that would bring the stranded, damaged ship back to Earth. They didn't know whether their efforts would succeed in bringing the Odyssey safely home, and they had no way of knowing until they tried it. And they had only one chance.

They had to throw away the flight plans that they spent years developing and practicing, and come up with a whole new plan, and do it as they went. They did not have the luxury of time to experiment, test, redesign, retry. It had to be right. The first time. They had seconds and minutes to do what they previously had months and years to accomplish. As each new problem arose, they had to develop a solution that would get the astronauts through.

The astronauts lost heat in the cabin and they didn't have enough safe water to drink. Their food became inedible. The levels of carbon dioxide were becoming dangerously high and they had to quickly come up with a makeshift system to remove it. Sleep was almost impossible because the temperature dropped to 38 degrees F. Condensation covered the walls. Since the power supply was critically low, they had to determine what equipment they needed to leave turned on, what could be turned off, and then calculate the exact sequence to power everything back up in order to conserve the power they had and have enough left to get them back to Earth.

A normal re–entry was accompanied by several minutes of communications blackout. Apollo 13's re-entry was originally calculated to be just over three minutes. But nothing about Apollo 13's re-entry was going to be normal or routine now.

When the spacecraft re–entered the earth's atmosphere, the friction of the spacecraft against the atmosphere would create extremely high temperatures and pressures. Because of the damage to the heat shield during the explosion no one knew if the spacecraft and the astronauts would survive the heat of re–entry. They had a checklist of more than 500 items that they had written only hours before. The oxygen, water and power levels were critical. In order to successfully enter Earth's atmosphere they had to perform an emergency trajectory correction maneuver to correct the direction of the spacecraft with a ship that was not designed to do that, and it had to be just right. Too shallow and they would bounce off, too deep and they would plummet to Earth. Added to that, a battery that was needed to release the parachutes for touchdown was predicted to fail just about the time the parachutes needed to come out.

No, this was definitely not routine.

They finally came up with an idea to execute the correction maneuver. They had to use power in order to do it. No room for mistakes. It had to put them on the right path and still leave them with enough power to get home.

Everyone held their breath.

The maneuver was successful, but no time to relax yet. Still a long way to go. Now they had to prepare for re–entry. They powered up Odyssey and moved from Aquarius back to Odyssey, they jettisoned Aquarius, and not long after Odyssey began its descent.

The communication blackout began.

One minute.

Two minutes.

Time passed so slowly.

Two minutes and 30 seconds.

The lead retro–fire officer said the blackout should be over in another 30 seconds. Thirty seconds later – nothing. Thirty seconds after that there was still no word from the astronauts.

The Capcom called for the crew to answer.

Silence.

Minds were racing through the possible scenarios - was the heat shield too damaged by the explosion? Had the gyros failed and caused the capsule to bounce off the atmosphere and hurl them into the oblivion of space or cause them to plunge to Earth in a fiery ball? Was their data correct? Had they overlooked anything? Had they forgotten something? There was nothing they could do but wait.

The seconds seemed like hours.

Four minutes.

They waited.

Five minutes.

And waited.

There was a moment – a very long moment – when it seemed that all was lost. They stood, and watched, and hoped. I'm certain many prayed.

Six minutes.

Then, at last, a recovery plane reported what they had all been working so hard and waiting so long for. It had picked up the radio signal of the command module – they were alive!

"Per my mission log it started at 142:39 and ended at 142:45 — a total of six minutes. Blackout was 1:27 longer than predicted.... Toughest minute and a half we ever had."

Gene Krantz, Apollo 13 flight director

But it wasn't time to celebrate. Mission control sat in silence. The astronauts were not home safe yet. The main parachutes still had to be deployed for them to safely touch down in the ocean, and the battery that was predicted to fail was the one that provided the power for the chutes to open. Did it survive the cold of space, the heat of re-entry?

Then – suddenly – the images of three orange and white parachutes unfolded gloriously into view on the screen!

Nine minutes later, at 12:07 PM on April 17, 1970, Odyssey safely touched water in the South Pacific Ocean. And only 4 miles from the prime recovery ship!

Mission control erupted into cheers.

Many cried.

> *God has blessed each of us with knowledge, wisdom, and the ability to think, reason, choose, and act on that wisdom and that knowledge*

The astronauts and crew at mission control had spent many long hours identifying, diagnosing, and working one life–threatening problem after another to bring Apollo 13 safely home.

Each one of those men and women were put in a situation where they had to find out just how much was in them. They drew on strength they were not aware they had. They drew on knowledge in a way they had not done previously. They came together, each giving their part to make the whole successful. They accomplished what no one had done before, and, thankfully, no one has had to do since.

But millions have benefited from what they did, from what was learned.

Apollo 13 is a vivid example of what can be done when we don't know something can be done. God has blessed each of us with knowledge, wisdom, and the ability to think, reason, choose, and act on that wisdom and that knowledge.

Now some of those men and women at mission control, to be sure, were intently, desperately, looking to God to give them the answers they so desperately needed, to give them the wisdom on how to draw on their years of training and education.

But not all had their eyes on God. Some were looking exclusively to their natural knowledge and abilities. Great as that knowledge and those abilities may be, they are still very limited. And yet, look at what they accomplished.

> *Imagine what you could accomplish if you were hooked up with the Creator Himself*

It stands today as a monument to what man can achieve.

What a triumph it was!

Now imagine for a minute what could be accomplished if an entire group of men and women came together and intentionally looked to God for the answers they needed to accomplish the task before them.

Imagine what could be if a group of men and women came together and, as one, looked to God for the dream He wanted them to fulfill.

Imagine if *you* looked to God for the dream He wants *you* to fulfill.

Imagine what *you* could accomplish if *you* were hooked up with the Creator Himself!

Imagine what *you* could accomplish if *you* were delivered from the constraints of the limitations and the limiting belief systems that have been imposed on you.

Imagine what *your* life would be like if *you* actually lived in the reality of limitlessness because of what Jesus has done for *you.*

It's *your* time to see your reality the way God sees it.

Imagine the possibilities!

Your time is now.

You have big dreams.

You have a bigger God.

CHAPTER TWO

6 – 10 %

IT'S BEEN SAID THAT we use 6 – 10 % of our brain.

Stop and think for a minute about all man has accomplished throughout history – like the space program, the Apollo mission we just talked about, all the medical breakthroughs, walking on the moon, the Space Station, photographing Mars, Saturn, and Neptune, bluetooth, cell phones, computers, or even the technological marvels of the pyramids from thousands of years ago.

All of the great things man has done have been done using only six to ten percent of his brain, only six to ten percent of his available capacity for intelligence, wisdom, and knowledge. Six to ten percent of his ability to know, understand and reason.

Let's take a look at the group called MENSA. "Mensa" is Latin for "table" and is an international roundtable organization. People can gather to exchange ideas, to research, and to socialize. It was founded in 1946 for people from all walks of life. It consists of professors, truck drivers, firefighters, police officers, artists. They range in age from 2 to 100, although most are between the ages of 20 and 60. At last report, there were approximately 110,000 members worldwide.[1] So what could such a diverse group of people possibly have in common? What brings them together?

Their common bond is their IQ. You are qualified to join Mensa if you have an IQ within the top 2% of the world's population. This is a group of the world's most intelligent people. The smartest of the smart. Their IQs are well above that of most people. Yet even the best of the best only use 6–10% of their brain. Some have said it can go as high as 15–20%.

Even the world's most intelligent people use only a fraction of their available capacity for knowledge and intelligence.

And the sad truth is that all of us, MENSA and non-MENSA, forget much of what we've learned.

> *Imagine what it would be like to hook up with the One Who created your brain in the first place*

What would the picture look like if we actually remembered everything we have ever learned, if we could tap into that knowledge reserve whenever we needed it?

What if we didn't have to relearn things over and over again?

What would your IQ be if you could use 30% of your brain? How much could you achieve if you regularly used 50% of your brain?

Imagine what would be possible if you could regularly use the other 90%. After you've thought about that for awhile, stop and think about this. Imagine what it would be like to hook up with the One Who created your brain in the first place! You know, the One Who knows all the ins and outs of how it's supposed to work, and work perfectly, all the time.

Do you have days when you feel sharper, more alert, more creative?

Do you have days when you are so productive, so efficient, that, at the end of the day, you are amazed at all you accomplished?

What if those days aren't just because you got a good night's sleep, but are possible because it is at those times that you are somehow using more of your brain than you normally use?

Maybe there are certain conditions that combine that allow us to tap into a greater percentage of our brains for brief periods.

Most of our brain is dormant most of the time. At least to us. But what if our entire brain was full of life, awake, active – all the time? What if we didn't just have "moments" of greater achievement, greater inspiration? What if those days were ordinary and not the exception? And what if being creative, productive and inspired just flowed effortlessly through our lives daily?

Now just imagine what your life would be like if you could walk hand–in–hand with the One Who created your brain in the first place. Well, the good news is – you can! You really can connect to the One Who created your brain, the One Who created everything about you. When you are united with the God Who made you, with the God Who created the universe and all the stars and the galaxies and all that we haven't discovered yet, your life takes on a whole new dimension.

> *In relationship with Jesus you are so much more than you were before*

You have a whole new frame of reference, and limitless possibilities to explore. When you walk and talk with the God of the universe, you will learn things so awesome, so extraordinary and exciting that you can't wait for the next thing He will show you. Tomorrow becomes very exciting. You were created for Him to love. He delights in having a relationship with you. He has you inscribed on the palm of His Hand. You are the apple of His Eye.[2]   He has so many things that He wants to show you and He is always excited to spend time with you.[3]

In relationship with Him, you are no longer limited to that 6–10%. You are so much more than you were before. He will show you things to encourage you, to inspire you, to teach you, to make you bigger on the inside so He can make you bigger on the outside.

It's His good pleasure to give you the Kingdom and He is waiting to reveal it to you.[4]

Expand.

Increase.

Imagine the possibilities!

God is bigger than the dream

He gave you

CHAPTER THREE

A WHOLE NEW LIFE
AWAKENED

BEFORE WE CONTINUE, let's take a minute to look at how we got here in the first place. I mean, if God created such a wonderful, complex thing as our brain, why can't we use it? Why does most of it just lay there?

You see, when Adam chose to submit to satan in the garden that day instead of to remain with God, he was cut off from the Life that made him. And he was cut off from pure Love.

He died that day, and man ever since has been born into that death and has lived in that death,[1] cut off from the Giver of Life. Some of the effects of that death are aging, sickness, poverty, physical death.

And our brains' process of "shutting down" is also one of the consequences of the death that entered that day. Actually, I believe it was God, in His mercy, closing off our brains to us so we would not destroy ourselves any more quickly than we already do, just as He divided the languages so man could not devise destructive, disastrous schemes.[2] We are all born into death and our thoughts are inherently evil, so He shut down our brains to keep us from accessing the ability to rapidly annihilate ourselves.

Remember that Adam was cut off not only from the Giver of Life but also from pure, real Love. Man's motives became selfish and prideful. Instead of following God's way, he was doing things his own way. Rather than putting others first and looking to their good, he was more inclined to put himself first and not be concerned about whether or not anyone got hurt along the way.

The gifts and abilities that God gave man – including his ability to think, reason, plan, and learn – were no longer under the control of the One Who is pure goodness and love and light. They were now under the control of the evil one – the god of this world – whose goal is to kill, steal and destroy the ones who look and act like God. Satan brings death to everything he touches. He brings destruction everywhere he is given permission to be involved. He perverts God's gifts, plans and purposes.

> *The cross changed everything*

Satan's war is with God, and his desire is to be exalted above God and draw the worship of man away from God and to himself through any avenue and any vehicle possible – through false doctrines, false teachers, false preachers, through music, media, politics, entertainment, and many more.[3]

But when Jesus came and paid the price for Adam's sin and gave us the ability to be restored to the life that was lost, everything changed. You could say that Jesus' death and resurrection was a game changer. The cross changed everything.

"When you were dead in your transgressions and the uncircumcision of your flesh, He made you alive together with Him, having forgiven us all our transgressions, having canceled out the certificate of debt consisting of decrees against us, which was hostile to us; and He has taken it out of the way, having nailed it to the cross. When He had disarmed the rulers and authorities, He made a public display of them, having triumphed over them through it."

Colossians 2:13 - 15

The rulers that He disarmed are those that have had control over us since that day in the garden. He triumphed over them in the cross.

Jesus paid the price so we no longer have to be controlled by that death.

There is a reason that Jesus says you must be born again to see the Kingdom of God. The phrase "kingdom of God" means the place of God's rule and dominion. He said that if we want to see God's rule and dominion in our lives, instead of being controlled by satan and death, then we must be born again.

The phrase "born again" is intentional – because that is exactly what happens. When you receive Jesus as Lord, you are born all over again. The first time you were born you were born into sin, death, defeat and destruction. When you are born again, you are born into life, liberty, love and God's kingdom. Everything you were before that moment died, and everything you are from that moment on is completely brand new, and everything you are from that moment on is of God.[4]

> *You really can live victoriously,*
> *prosperously, productively*

You have begun a whole new life with a whole new way of thinking and a whole new way of doing things and looking at things.

And now God Himself – pure love and perfect life - has come to dine with you. You are in Him and He is in you. Cell by cell, breath by breath, you are now one with Him.

Jesus made it all possible.

Now you can hear His voice, know His thoughts. He has given you His Spirit so you can know all truth, know all things, and remember everything Jesus has ever said to you.[5]

And guess what – by the Holy Spirit you really can access all He is so you can be all you are intended to be.[6] You really can tap into the other 90%.

And even better than that – you are now hooked up to the One Who made the whole 100% in the first place! You really can live victoriously,

prosperously,

productively.

Supernatural can be natural for you.

Imagine the possibilities.

Your time really is now.

Where will you be next year

if you started your journey

today?

CHAPTER FOUR

MOVING FORWARD

HIS PEACE NEVER LEAVES

GOD HAS PROVIDED A WAY for us to have confidence in our dreams and our imaginations.

He has given us freedom to be all He created us to be. He has given us His peace to abide with us. He is the One Who is at work in us both to desire His good pleasure and to accomplish His good pleasure.[1]

He told us, *"Let not your heart be troubled. Believe in God, believe also in Me."*[2] And then He said, *"Peace I leave with you; My peace I give to you; not as the world gives do I give to you."*[3] "World" here means "world-ruler," and is used as an insulting way to refer to satan. Jesus said that He did not give us the same peace that the world–ruler gives. That kind of peace is fleeting – here one minute and gone the next. He gave us His peace, the same peace that He had with the Father from the foundation of the world. The peace He has given us never leaves, never changes. It abides. It is eternal.

> *He has given us freedom to be all He created us to be*

He gave us peace of mind, quietness, rest, tranquility – all possible because we have been reconciled to God. Being in a state of peace does not mean the absence of conflict or problems. It is that state of knowing the ultimate outcome of victory, a revelation of being completely and totally accepted and loved by God, and the knowledge that Heaven itself is there to protect, defend and fight for you.

Now the scripture says that we are to *"let the peace of Christ rule in our hearts."*[4] So let's dig a little deeper into that. The phrase "our hearts" refers to the center or the seat of our thoughts, desires, feelings, affections, passions, and impulses. The word translated "rule" here is from the Greek word meaning to decide, to determine, to direct, to control, and it involves continuous, repeated action.

So, here is what He said:

"Let His quietness, tranquility, rest, and peace of mind continually and repeatedly decide, determine, direct and control your thoughts, desires, feelings, affections, passions and impulses."

Sounds kind of complete, doesn't it?
Thorough.
Permanent.
However, we have been taught things that have confused the issue and robbed us of that peace.

I had always been taught, and so I had always believed, that the way to know if we are making the right decision or going the right way is that we will feel His peace. We will have that moment of peace deep inside and will know whether something is right or not. When we feel His peace, we know we're doing the right thing.

> *He has given us His peace, and that peace abides*

But then the Lord showed me something I hadn't seen before. That way of thinking assumes that the rest of the time we are somehow not in complete peace, that we live at some level in a state of disquiet and a sense of uneasiness. Deep peace comes only when we make a right decision or take the right path.

But, as we just learned, He wants constant peace for us. The peace He has given us never leaves, and we have peace with God because of what Jesus has done for us. There is no longer anything between us and the Father to separate us or condemn us.[5] His intention is for us to live and remain in His peace continually.

So then what does it mean to let the peace of Christ rule in our heart? How do we make that real in our everyday lives? He showed me that rather than leading us by a sense of peace He leads us more by a sense of disquiet. If we are making a wrong decision, if we are heading in the wrong direction, we sense an uneasiness. It is those times when we sense that uneasiness that we know that there is something not right about the choice we are making or the direction we are going. His peace doesn't leave us, but there is a disquiet that sort of overlays our peace. He wants us to be sensitive to that sense of disquiet and obey His leading for us.

We also need to discern whether that disquiet is His leading, or whether it is our own reluctance to obey. We may simply be afraid to take that step that God wants us to take. We need discernment from the Holy Spirit to know which one. If we're not sure, all we have to do is ask for wisdom, and He will bring clarity and confirmation.[6] Of course, if the decision we are making or the step we are taking is in direct disobedience to His written Word, then that is our answer. We need no discernment beyond what He has already said in His Word. If He said in His Word not to do something, there is no reasoning, no rationalizing that will remove that uneasiness and disquiet. If we continue to go our own way in disobedience to His written Word, all we can do is ignore that uneasiness, bury it, try to put it behind us, and even gather to ourselves teachers, preachers and friends that will agree with us. What happens then is our hearts become hardened to the voice of the Lord and the leading of the Spirit. But once we admit our mistake and repent of our disobedience, our hearts are restored because we are once again in agreement with Him.

Now I want to deal with another common teaching that robs us of our peace, keeps us bound by fear and keeps us from stepping out boldly in what He has told us to do, and that is that we can get ahead of God.

Moving forward in His peace we are free to fulfill His plans for us. Jesus told us that all authority in Heaven and in Earth has been given to Him. And then He gave us the use of His Name and said that, in that authority, we are to go into all the world, do the works that He did and make disciples of every nation.

That's what Paul did.

That's what Peter did.

> *To wait for the Lord means to twist together, to bind together, to hope*

The teaching that discourages us from taking bold steps, from moving forward with what God has told us to do, is that we are told to wait on God before making a move because we don't want to get ahead of God or make a mistake.

It puts us in fear.

What does the phrase "wait for God" or "wait on God" really mean? In Psalm 27, verse 14, it says, *"wait for the Lord, be strong and let your heart take courage. Yes, wait for the Lord."* Again, in Psalm 37, verse 7, we read, *"Rest in the Lord and wait patiently for Him."* There are many times the phrases *"wait on the Lord"* and *"wait for the Lord"* are used in the Old Covenant.

> *Under the New Covenant we are one with Him*

To wait for the Lord means to twist together, to bind together, to hope.

Isn't that great? Waiting on God means to bind yourself to Him, to twist yourself together with Him, to hope in Him. Another really interesting thing is that the phrases "wait on God" and "wait for the Lord" are not used in the New Testament, except where it says to wait for Jesus to come to judge others. (NASB)

Why?

Because it means to twist together with Him. Under the Old Covenant, man did not have a vital relationship with God. They were cut off from Him and separated from Him. They knew Him and worshipped Him from a distance. They had mediators between them and God. But under the New Covenant, when we are born again, we are one with Him. We no longer have any mediator between us and God except Jesus. There is no longer any need to bind ourselves together with Him because we are already completely, thoroughly, and permanently united with Him and one with Him. When we renew our minds to that truth, we are transformed, our entire outlook changes.

So, we've been admonished to wait on God in fear of getting ahead of Him. Then one day, while I was doing the dishes, the Lord asked me, "When did I say it was possible to get ahead of Me?"

That really took me by surprise. I mean, I was just standing there, minding my own business, washing my dishes. But I had to admit I had never really thought about it. I just accepted that we could get ahead of Him because I heard so many people teach that we could. So He began to show me what He has to say about it. What a concept!

First of all, getting ahead of God implies that, somehow, I am able to outrun, outthink or outsmart Him, that I am somehow able to move faster than He is able to move and get somewhere before He does, outrunning His ability to cover me with His grace and guide my steps.

The teaching to keep me from getting ahead of God is intended keep me in submission to God at all times, to obediently follow His ways and instructions rather than selfishly or disobediently taking off on my own. Now that sounds good. Aren't we supposed to submit to God and obey Him? Without question. Isn't He smarter than we are? Absolutely!

But that kind of thinking, though not intended to do so, puts the focus on me, puts me in the center. It says that my ability to run ahead in the wrong direction or at the wrong time is somehow greater than Jesus' ability to correct and direct me. It makes me self occupied. It creates in me a fear – a fear that I will "miss it," a fear that I will make a mistake, a fear that I will mess things up. It focuses on what I can do, what I did or should have done, what I shouldn't do or shouldn't have done. It focuses on my choices, my actions, my mistakes – me, me, me.

It puts me back into the same mindset as those under the law in the Old Covenant. The law is about the works of man. It says, "Thou shall not." "Thou shall not." "Thou shall not." It is "me" focused. It causes me to be focused on all the things I am not allowed to do and all the things I am supposed to do to please God. If I miss it, God won't be pleased with me. I won't be blessed.

The law makes you self focused.

Grace makes you Jesus focused.

The Word tells us that if we are under law, we are no longer under grace, which also means that if we are under grace, we are no longer under law. (See Galatians 5:18, Romans 6:14; 8:2, 12-17) The New Covenant of grace is all about the works of God through Christ Jesus, the works of God on our behalf. It is about His love for us. The Word says that perfect love casts out fear. Not our perfect love for Him – because our love can never be perfect, but His perfect love for us – because His love is always perfect. So when we meditate on how much God loves us, fear leaves.

Religion and our society have made us very self focused. Religion teaches us that it is up to us to behave just the right way in order to please God and receive His blessings and answers to our prayers. Society tells us that it is up to us to change ourselves so we can excel.

If you go to any good bookstore, you will find a section called something like "Self-Improvement." There you'll find all kinds of books describing various principles, rules and methods you can follow to improve yourself. In all these books, the focus is on *you* using *your* willpower and *your* self-discipline to apply the principles to improve yourself. Many life coaches today do the same. They make *you* the complete focus – what life do *you* want, what do *you* want to get, what do *you* want to achieve. A good coach will point you to Jesus and what He wants you to do, what He has for you, and what He already has done in you and for you, and how to walk that out in your life. That is the only place you will ever find real success and fulfillment. God does not want you focusing on yourself. Your willpower and determination can only take you so far, with results that last only as long as your willpower lasts or until you hit a wall that your determination cannot get past. God has a higher way. He wants you to be Jesus–occupied. When you look to yourself to improve yourself, you are putting confidence in your flesh. But the Bible tells us that in our flesh dwells no good thing (Romans 7:18), and that we should put no confidence in our flesh (Philippians 3:3).

"Some boast in chariots and some in horses, But we will boast in the name of the LORD, our God."   Psalm 20:7

My friend, the best way to change yourself is stop being self occupied and be occupied with Jesus. When you read the Bible see His beauty, His majesty, His love, His compassion and His grace. As you keep beholding and meditating on Him and His glory, the Holy Spirit inside you goes to work in you. He will transform you into the very same image of Christ. You will be changed from glory to glory, experiencing true transformation that lasts!

"But we all, with unveiled face, beholding as in a mirror the glory of the Lord, are being transformed into the same image from glory to glory, just as from the Lord, the Spirit."

2 Cor 3:18

On the cross Jesus paid the full price for us, and we are no longer under the law – the ministry of death. We are now under grace – the ministry of righteousness.[7] The Old Covenant was based on us doing something so that God could then do something. The New Covenant is based on us being able to do something because of what Jesus has already done. Instead of hearing, "Thou shall not," "Thou shall not," "Thou shall not," God now says, "I will." "I will." "I will." Instead of God telling us what *we* can't do, He now tells us what *He* will do.

"*I will be a God to them.*"

"*I will cause them to walk in My ways.*"

"*I will remember their sins no more.*"

Read Hebrews 8:10-13 and see how many times God says "I will."

We are no longer living in the separation from God that began in the garden of Eden. We are now in perfect union with our Father because of what Jesus did for us on the cross. We are not sinners. We are sons. We are not servants in the house. We are the heirs of the household. The cross really did change everything.

The cross split time in two.

BC – AD

Because of Jesus, we have received the abundance of His grace and the gift of righteousness. Under the New Covenant of grace, the focus is completely, exclusively, entirely on Jesus.

Period.

We are one with Him. We know His voice. He leads us by His Spirit. He trusts us. His desire is for us to see ourselves as He sees us.

Have you read the verse in the book of Acts where the disciples were making plans and deciding on what to do? They said, "*it seemed good to the Holy Spirit and to us...*" [8] That is the union we have with Him. He is right here, with us, working with us, helping us.

Always.

He wants our focus, first and foremost, to be on His love for us, and not to be afraid that we're going to miss it.

> *It's impossible for me to go somewhere that He does not go!*

Then He pointed out to me that if I can somehow get ahead of Him, it suggests that He stays behind and watches me go on ahead. But He said that He'd never leave me, which means that while I'm running on ahead, He's right there, keeping step with me. He's one with me, I'm one with Him. It's impossible for me to go somewhere that He does not go! (See Psalm 139)

His Word says that no matter where we go, God is there. He knows our thoughts, and before we even speak a word He knows what we're going to say. Nothing can separate us from His love. He knows the end from the beginning. Jesus is the first and the last, which means that nothing that happens takes Him by surprise.[9]

We are one with Him.

> *We have come up with a lot of doctrines and traditions designed to keep us in our living room when God wants us to go into all the world*

So, really, how is it possible to "get ahead of Him?"

We've been told to wait until He tells us to go. The scriptures actually teach just the opposite.

Instead of waiting until He tells us to go, He has told us to go until He tells us to stop. He's big enough to deal with us. If we are not living in rebellion, if our heart and mind are set on Him and our eyes look to Him, He is free to direct us. If we are living in rebellion to Him, then we have other issues to deal with. And remember, Jesus told us not to be fearful, but to believe on Him as we do the

Father. If we make a mistake, He will lovingly get us back on track. The steps of the righteous are ordered by the Lord and He delights in his way.[10]

We have come up with a lot of doctrines and traditions designed to keep us in our living room when God wants us to go into all the world. We have invalidated the Word of God by our traditions.[11] We do not have a full revelation of sonship.

His Word says that the gates of Hades will not prevail against us – they will not be able to hold up against our advances as we come against what satan is doing – He wants us on offense. Yet many believers live the other way around – holding on so Hades won't break through their gates. They're constantly on defense.

Jesus gave us the authority to use His Name and gave us authority over all the power of the enemy so that nothing would hurt us, and told us to go into all the world and said He would be with us always. By Jesus we reign in life, and God always causes us to triumph through Jesus. He has seated us with Jesus in heavenly places far above all rule and power and dominion and every name that is named.[12] Yet we live our lives as if that were not so. We live in fear of the evil one and his schemes, in fear of making a mistake. We have more faith in what could go wrong than we do in what Jesus has done and in what God has told us to do.

God gave the earth to man and gave us dominion over all the work of His hands – over everything He made. He brought the animals to Adam to see what he would name them, and the scripture says, *"And whatever the man called a living creature that was its name."* God did not say, *"Whatever I tell you to call them, that shall be their name."* Instead He said *"whatever Adam called them, that was their name."* He left it completely up to Adam.[13] Those names stand to this day.

Let's look at Paul.

He was preaching the word and strengthening the churches in city after city. They passed through the Galatian and Phyrgian regions, *"having been forbidden by the Holy Spirit to speak the Word in Asia."*

Acts 16:6

And again, when they had come to a place called Mysia, they were trying to go into Bithynia, and *"the Spirit of Jesus did not permit them."*

Acts 16:7

They did not wait until the Spirit told them to go, but went until the Holy Spirit told them to stop.[14] Let's look at another incident in Paul's life. He handled things somewhat differently than many Christians would. He had a revelation of the new birth and grace and understood the partnership of the Holy Spirit. In the book of Acts the Holy Spirit records that one night Paul had a dream – a vision in the night – of a man in Macedonia calling to him to come to Macedonia to help them. *Immediately* Paul and those with him sought to go into Macedonia, concluding that God had called them to preach the gospel there. While there, they were beaten and thrown into prison. (Acts 16)

Now that would have played out quite differently in the lives of many believers today. Today many would report the vision to those around them and say something like, "Pray and intercede for Macedonia because God is going to send us there one day." And again, in light of the problems Paul and Silas faced while in Macedonia, much of the counsel from other believers would be something like, "You got ahead of God." "You didn't wait on Him for His timing, that's why you had those problems." "If it's God's will and His timing, you wouldn't have had any obstacles," or "If it's God's will everything will just flow." Problems and obstacles don't mean we are out of God's will, but rather could mean just the opposite – that we are doing exactly what God wants us to do and satan is trying to stop us. Remember how he had all the babies killed when Moses was born, and again when Jesus was born? If we allow our circumstances to determine for us whether or not we are in the will of God, we will seldom ever be there.

Look at another circumstance in Paul's life: *"For we wanted to come to you – I, Paul, more than once – and yet satan hindered us."*

1 Thes 2:18

So we see that there are times when the Holy Spirit restrains and other times when satan hinders. We need to discern which it is, and not just assume that because there are problems that we are out of God's will. If the absence of problems, delays or obstacles are how we determine whether we are in God's will and timing, then we have to conclude that neither Jesus nor Paul were constantly in the center of God's will. They encountered difficulties and opposition frequently. They also offended many.

We definitely have a different way of looking at things today than the first century believers did.

I pray that we, each one, pray for the courage to be who we are and step out into the world and do our part to establish the kingdom of God in the earth.

"'And now, Lord, take note of their threats, and grant that Thy bondservants may speak Your Word with all confidence, while Thou dost extend Thy Hand to heal, and signs and wonders take place through the Name of Thy

Holy Servant Jesus.' And when they had prayed, the place where they had gathered together was shaken, and they were all filled with the Holy Spirit and began to speak the Word of God with boldness."   Acts 4:29-31

Notice that they didn't shrink back because of the threats, but instead asked God to bless them to be bold and speak His Word in spite of whatever opposition they encountered. They did not wait for a more opportune time when things would be easier. Nor did they ask God to take away the difficulties. And God answered and sent His power, just as they asked.

"But My righteous one shall live by faith; and if he shrinks back My Soul has no pleasure in Him."   Heb 10:38

So then if our focus is on God's love for us and our desire is to do His will, and we are willing to go until He tells us to stop, we will know the disquiet of the restraint of the Holy Spirit concerning a wrong plan or a wrong path, just as Paul did. We can ask for His wisdom if we're not sure if the uneasiness is that He is directing us another way, or our own fear of doing something new and unfamiliar. Paul could have easily ignored the Holy Spirit and gone ahead with his plans to go into those towns that the Holy Spirit told Him not to. So can we. Paul could have easily retreated in the face of all the obstacles he encountered. So can we. And like Paul and the first century believers we, too, have the very same power to go and do all He has given us to accomplish in spite of the problems.

"The people who know their God will display strength and take action." Daniel 11:32

Let your sails catch the wind of the Holy Spirit. Keep your compass set on the Son. He won't let you get off course.

Moving forward.

Moving on.

Your time is now.

Pray big, ask big, dream big ~

God can handle it

CHAPTER FIVE

HERE'S WHY YOU CAN

WHEN YOU ARE BORN AGAIN, you become a child of God. You are no longer your own. You were bought with a price. It is no longer you who live but Christ Who lives in you, and the life you live now you live by the faith of the Son of God.[1]

As a child of God you are now one with Him. You are so united with Him that it is no longer possible to separate the two of you. You can no longer tell where one ends and the other begins. Like when a drop of blue dye has been added to a gallon of water – the whole gallon of water turns blue and that one drop of color fills the whole gallon of water. The blue can no longer be taken out of the water, and the water can no longer be separated from the drop of dye. You, God the Father, Jesus Christ the Son and the Holy Spirit are not side–by–side. You are one. God is in you, You are in Him. Forever.[2]

> *In Jesus we have the forgiveness of our sins – past, present, future*

You have His Name, His Mind, His DNA (Divine Nature and Attributes). And He has given you the Holy Spirit to reveal to you those things that He has freely given to you.[3]

The salvation you have from Him is more than the forgiveness of sins, though that is pretty awesome. The forgiveness of sins makes the new birth possible. On the cross Jesus took away the sin – the power that exerts itself on mankind that is in opposition to God, and He paid the penalty for the acts of sin that are born out of that power that separated us from God. Jesus became sin and took on Himself all of God's wrath against that sin.

God's wrath was not against man but against the sin that separated Him from the man He loves. On the cross Jesus said, *"Father, forgive them. They know not what they do."* He knew that all of mankind was victim of the sin they were born into. We did not choose to be born into death, but now we do have a choice. We can choose to be born again into the life we were created to have!

In Jesus we have the forgiveness of our sins – past, present, future.

The forgiveness of your sins makes it possible for you to receive salvation, to be born again and to become a child of God, to be reunited with God, to become His heir and receive His Kingdom. Salvation means

saved,

delivered,

protected,

healed,

made whole,

kept safe.

"But as many as received Him, to them He gave the right to become children of God, even to those who believe in His Name"   John 1:12

Jesus' death, burial, and resurrection tell the whole story.

When God created Adam and Eve and placed them in the garden they had everything they needed. They walked and talked with God. Adam named all the animals, and the names he gave them remain to this day. He used all 100% of his brain.

Then, when Adam turned his back on God and joined himself to satan, he was cut off from Life. He no longer had the same relationship with God Who gave him his life, with God Who was his life. His body and his environment immediately began to feel the consequences of being cut off from Life. Creation itself was subjected to futility when Adam submitted himself to satan. (Romans 8:20-22)

"Cursed is the ground because of you"

Genesis3:17

When Adam walked and talked with God he had everything he needed. His food was right there for him to eat – the trees were full of fruit and all he had to do was pick it. The ground was lush and fertile. Mist rose from the ground and watered it. The ground was full of gold and precious stones.[4] God is so good! He thinks of everything!

Then after Adam bowed to satan, giving permission for him to be in charge and for sin to enter the garden and he was cut off from Life, one of the results was that he hid himself in fear from the God he once walked and talked with[5] (how sad!), and instead of simply picking his food from the abundant supply of the trees in the garden, he now had to toil, labor and sweat to grow his food.[6]

So, through all the years from Adam to Jesus, man was essentially separated from God. God made a way for him to be covered and protected through the law of Moses and the blood of bulls and goats, but there was no true, vital relationship. The Holy Spirit would come upon people but He did not stay. David prayed that God would not take His Holy Spirit from him. God gave the people prophets to let them know what He wanted to say to them because they could not hear Him for themselves as Adam once could. In fact when God did speak, the people said it was thunder (John 12), and when Moses had been in God's presence and his face shone, the people were afraid. (Exodus 34) When God's presence was on the mountain, the people were afraid that they would die and told Moses to speak with God and tell them what He said. (Deuteronomy 5)

> *He didn't want to be just Creator to His creatures. He wanted to be Father to His children*

What a stark difference in man's relationship with God from before Adam's fall!

God knew what was going to happen in the garden between Adam and the serpent – He knows the end from the beginning. Adam's fall did not take Him by surprise. But before He even created the heavens and the earth, God had a plan all worked out to restore His relationship with His man.[7] You see, the garden of Eden was not God's goal –

the marriage supper of the Lamb was His goal. And God knew that He would have to go through the garden to get to the marriage supper.

He didn't want to be just Creator to His creatures. He wanted to be Father to His children. He is love, and love needs an object. He wanted to love on man and for that man to receive His love. And He had a plan.

That plan was Jesus. The Christ. The Messiah. Emmanuel. God with us. Jesus was crucified from the foundation of the world. (Revelation 13, KJV) He knew going in what was going to happen and what it would cost Him. But because of His great love for us, He was willing to do whatever it took to restore His relationship with us.

And God already has a plan in place to fix what's broken in your life. That plan is Jesus. The Christ. The Messiah. Emmanuel. God with us.

At the right time, Jesus came to buy us back from the control of satan, to pay the ransom needed for our deliverance, and make a way for us to be reunited with our God and Father.

Jesus was wounded and bruised because of our iniquities and transgressions.

He was scourged so we could be healed.

He was chastised so we could have peace with God.

The wrath of God against sin fell completely, totally, and once–and–for–all on Him. He fulfilled the law, and His death was the end of the law for us. He was made sin, died, and He descended into hell.

God raised Him from the dead when we were justified – He was raised from the dead when we were made as though there never was sin. He ascended to Heaven and cleansed the items of worship there, sat down at the right hand of the Father, and made it possible for us to come before the throne of God freely, confidently, without fear, to get help whenever we need it.[8] The veil between us and God was torn in two from top to bottom. God Himself tore it.

Jesus became sin, paid the price for our sins, fulfilled the law that was against us,[9] and He justified us – made us as if we never sinned. He was made sin and we were made His righteousness and He made our reunion with God possible.

> *Because of what Jesus has done for us we can now know God as Father*

Jesus took away our sins so we could be saved. He took away sin that entered the garden that day so we could be reunited with our God. When we acknowledge Jesus as Lord and believe that God raised Him from the dead – when we confess out loud Jesus as Lord and believe that we have been justified because of Jesus' resurrection – we are saved.[10] The word "saved" here is the Greek word "sozo" and it means to save, deliver, protect, heal, make whole, to be kept safe. It covers every area of our life and includes everything we will ever need.

Now a really cool thing here is this: when God restores, He always restores more, restores better, than what was lost.[11]

> *As born-again ones, we have the privilege, the honor, and the right to come to God as no other people in history have been able to do*

Remember that God's goal was always the marriage supper of the Lamb? Adam had a relationship with God. He walked and talked with Him. He knew God as his creator, his provider, his companion. And that's pretty great!

From the beginning in the garden God progressively revealed His Name to man so man could get to know more and more about Him. Adam knew Him as Creator, and to Moses He introduced Himself as YAHWEH - I AM THAT I AM, the existent One. Each one of God's Names reveals a different aspect of His character, tells us more about Who He is, and helps us understand how we can relate to Him, Who and What He is to us, and what He wants to be for us.

The Names He was known by under the Old Covenant are:

> Elohim – Creator
>
> Adonai – The Lord
>
> El Shaddai – The All-Sufficient One
>
> El Elyon – The God Most High
>
> El Roi –The God Who Sees

Jehovah, YAHWEH – The Self-Existent One

Jehovah–Jireh – The Lord is Provision

Jehovah–Rapha – The Lord is Health

Jehovah–Mekoddishkem – The Lord is Sanctification

Jehovah–Shalom – The Lord is Peace

Jehovah–Raah – The Lord is Shepherd

Jevovah–Tsidkenu – The Lord is Righteousness

Jehovah–Shammah – The Lord is There

Jehovah–Nissi – The Lord is My Banner

Jehovah–Sabaoth – The Lord of Hosts

It was by these names that the people under the Old Covenant knew God.

Now, because of what Jesus has done for us, we can once again walk and talk with God, know Him as creator, provider and companion. But we have more. He has given us the right to become His children.

We can now know the God and Creator of the universe as Father.

We are the bride of Christ![12]

When Jesus came, He revealed God to the world as He had never before been known. Jesus came and for the first time since the creation of the world revealed God as Father. He constantly referred to God as His Father, and then He revealed God to us as our Father.[13]

After He rose from the dead He told Mary, *"I ascend to My Father and to your Father, to My God and your God."* John 20:17

As born-again ones, we have the privilege, the honor, and the right to come to God as no other people in history have been able to do. We can boldly go before the throne of grace and call on Him as Father![14] When you are born again, put yourself into His Hands.

Completely

Totally

Without reservation

After all, you've already trusted Him with your eternity. Surely He can handle your time here on Earth. He is the One Who is at work in you to desire and to accomplish His desire, His plans.[15]   Remember, He is the One Who put the gifts, talents and passions in you. The more you agree with God about who you now are, the more you will be transformed into that new person.[16] His desires will begin to be your desires. The salvation you have from Him is for everything you will ever need or desire. He is able to do exceeding abundantly beyond all we ask or think. He does it according to the power that works in us.

> *Go ahead and dream big! God can handle it.*

That power is the Holy Spirit – the promise of the Father, whom the Father has sent in Jesus' Name. It is the same power that raised Jesus from the dead and gives life to our mortal bodies.[17] He has given us the Holy Spirit to reveal to us all that God has freely given us and it is our Father's pleasure to give us the Kingdom! Then He tells us to ask, seek, and knock and we will receive, we will find, and it will be opened up to us.[18]

So then, if He is able to do exceeding abundantly beyond what we can ask or even think – not just exceeding, but exceeding *abundantly beyond* – over and above, more than is necessary, surpassing, uncommon, excessive – then go ahead and dream big! God can handle it.

He wants us to work out our salvation with fear and trembling – work out what He has put in us with awe and wonder. Not *work for,* but *work out.* It's all in us and He wants us to work it out, like opening a new present every day. All that we are is new, all the old has passed away – it died when we made Jesus Lord. Everything in us now is new and is from God Himself.[19] Explore. Discover. Work out what He's put in you.

With awe and wonder.

> *God's grace is so great – He does it for us, He does it in us, He gives us the power to do it, then blesses us for doing it!*

Are you beginning to see the full circle? God made it, God gave it to Adam, Adam gave it to satan, Jesus bought it back, Jesus gave it back to us.

"In Him you have been made complete, and He is the head over all rule and authority." Colossians 2:10

"Rule" in this verse means from the beginning of all things. It means princes and chiefs among angels and among demons.

"Authority" means to have dominion, and refers also to those given power as rulers in heaven and hell – the princes, angels, archangels, and demons.

When we were dead in our sins, God made us alive together with Jesus, He forgave us all our sins, He canceled out the certificate of decrees that were against us, He disarmed the rulers and powers that had control over us since the garden, and triumphed over them in the cross. He made us complete and whole, and He is the head of all princes, angels, archangels, and demons. He gave us His Name and told us to go into all the world and do the works that He did, and said He would be with us always.

"When you were dead in your transgressions and the uncircumcision of your flesh, He made you alive together with Him, having forgiven us all our transgressions. Having canceled out the certificate of debt consisting of decrees against us and which was hostile to us; and He has taken it out of the way, having nailed it to the Cross. When He disarmed the rulers and authorities, He made a public display of them, having triumphed over them through it."

Colossians 2:13-15

"For this reason also, God highly exalted Him, and bestowed on Him the name which is above every name, so that at the name of Jesus every knee shall bow, of those who are in heaven and on earth and under the earth, and that every tongue will confess that Jesus Christ

is Lord, to the glory of God the Father."
Phil 2:9–11

"And He said to them, 'Go into all the world and preach the gospel to all creation.'"

Mark 16:15

"And Jesus came up and spoke to them, saying, 'All authority has been given to Me in heaven and on earth. Go therefore and make disciples of all the nations, baptizing them in the name of the Father and the Son and the Holy Spirit, teaching them to observe all that I commanded you; and lo, I am with you always, even to the end of the age.'"

Matthew 28:18-20

God's grace is so great – He does it for us, He does it in us, He gives us the power to do it, then blesses us for doing it! Is our Father an amazing God or what!

So now look to Him to show you what He has for you. Look to Him to open up your heart and mind so you can see beyond where you are now to all the tomorrows He still wants to show you.

He rejoices over you. He sings over you. He delights in you.

Imagine the possibilities.

Go for it!

Your time is now.

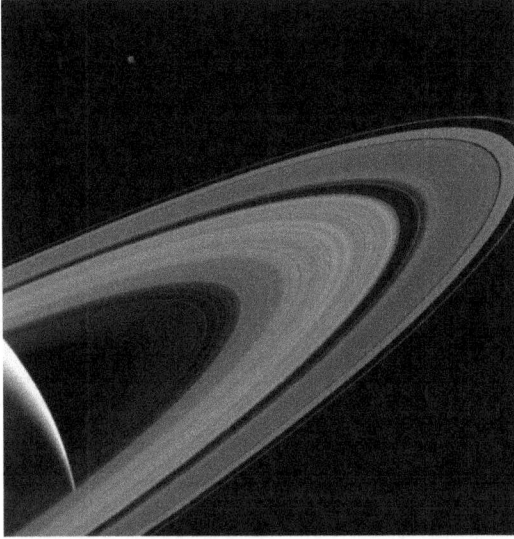

If you have the ability to

accomplish your dream,

you aren't dreaming

God's dream for you

CHAPTER SIX

FREE TO DREAM

HE MADE THE WAY

TO DREAM IS THE ABILITY to
imagine what could be.

Alexander Graham Bell was a dreamer.

When he was only 29 years old he invented
the telephone. He started the Bell Telephone
Company a year later – at the age of 30.

He did what had never been done before.

What he did endures to this day.

Colonel Sanders was 46 when he developed
his secret chicken recipe. When he was 66 he
began to sell franchises based on that secret
recipe. At that time, selling franchises was a
relatively new business. It was not as tried
and true as it is today. He didn't have a great

deal of knowledge or experience to rely on, no tested pattern to follow, not too many people to turn to for advice. He did what had never been done before.

> *You are never too old or too young to accomplish the dream God has given you*

Then, at the age of 87, he testified before the U.S. House of Representatives Subcommittee on Aging. He testified *against* mandatory retirement!

29 - 30 - 46 - 66 - 87 – you are never too old or too young to accomplish the dream God has given you.

Your time is now.

Dreams are one of the avenues God has given us to circumvent the limitations of our

natural knowledge. You know – that 6–10%.
It's one of the ways God makes it possible for
us to tap into that other 90%, to tap into His
heart and His mind.

So, what does it mean to dream? Does it
mean to while away the hours while life
passes you by?

Are dreams the adventures you experience
while asleep at night?

> *Since the fall in the garden,*
> *God's creation has been perverted*
> *at every level*

Is dreaming something you have been told
to avoid so you can stay focused on the
business of life, stay focused on "reality"? The
truth is God gave you the ability to dream.
Your imagination is actually a gift from God
Himself.

Now it's true that man's imagination has been corrupted. It has been used for devising evil schemes, for impurity, for countless ways of simply wasting time, and much more.

Since the fall in the garden, God's creation has been perverted at every level.

Take marriage for example. God's plan for marriage is quite different from what we have seen throughout history and especially what we see in the earth today.

First of all, after the fall in the garden God had to institute the law of marriage so men and women would remain together as husband and wife. The meaning of the word marriage is "a legal contract between a man and a woman to unite for life to the exclusion of all." It is a relationship bound by a law.

From the beginning it was never God's intention to make the uniting of a man and a woman into a law. In the beginning, before the fall, it was not necessary.

> *God never intended for something He created to be so beautiful to destroy the man He loves so much*

It was because of the fall, because man chose to make himself the focus of his life, to go his own way instead of continuing in God's way, because he submitted to satan and to sin, that his desires and his affections became perverted. It became necessary for marriage to be made a law because without a law a man would not remain with one wife. He would go from woman to woman. Without a law, a woman would not remain with one husband. She would go from man to man. God had to make the union between a man and a woman a law so we would not destroy ourselves.

God always knew what we have since learned – that sexual promiscuity brings destruction, both emotionally and physically. It causes depression, insecurity and fear as well as incurable sicknesses and diseases that many die from. There are new STDs being discovered all the time and the medical community is scrambling to try to find treatments and cures, yet the diseases rage on, bringing devastation and destruction.

We now have men and women casually and randomly having sex with anybody they want. Our children are being taught, not about abstinence and purity, but how to have safe sex – which is itself a lie of satan. We have homosexuality accepted and taught as normal, and a month celebrating LGBT history. We have redefined a monogamous relationship as having sex with only one person at a time. We have come up with a whole new relationship – "friends with benefits". The definition of "taking your relationship to the next level" means moving in together, assuming it is a step up, a step to more commitment. In reality it is a major step down toward the destruction that awaits. Sin always leads to death.

"The wages of sin is death, but the free gift of God is eternal life in Christ Jesus our Lord."
Romans 8:23

And we see everywhere the manifestations of that death – sterility, mental illness, cancers, pedophilia, STDs, impotence, rape, broken homes and broken children, incurable sickness, early death, loss of peace, security, trust and fulfillment. And so much more.

God never intended for something that He created to be so beautiful to destroy the man that He loves so much. God knew that sex used in ways He never intended would result in man's destruction. And, in His love for mankind, He desired to protect man from his desires that were now perverted.

Secondly, God never intended divorce. But the Bible says that because of man's hardness of heart, and because of God's grace, He permitted it. But Jesus said it was not this way from the beginning.[1]

Now there was a time when a group of religious leaders called Sadducees were questioning Jesus about the resurrection and who a certain woman would be married to in the resurrection if she had seven husbands on Earth. The Sadducees didn't believe in the resurrection and were trying to trap Him. Jesus answered them saying that they asked the question because they did not understand the scriptures or the power of God. He then went on to teach them that in the resurrection man will neither marry nor be given in marriage, but will be like the angels in heaven.[2]

Now many believe, since Jesus said there will be no marriage in heaven, that men and women will have completely different relationships with each other than they do now. They believe that there will not be the same intimacy as there is now. They will be friends, companions, etc, but no intimacy, no more conceiving and bearing children, God's command to them to be fruitful and multiply would cease. But, if that is true, what does knowing the power of God have to do with it? If it's different, it's just different. What part does God's power play?

> *Remember that God always restores more, not less*

Remember the Word "marriage" refers to a law. The Sadducees were assuming that in the resurrection mankind is unchanged. They didn't understand the scriptures. They didn't believe in the resurrection. Jesus pointed them to the power of God. That power is the power, the right, for man to become a child of God. See John 1:12. It was the power of God that raised Jesus from the dead, justifying man and delivering him from the grip of satan.

In the garden, before sin entered, God made them male and female and said, *"For this reason"* – because they were male and female – *"man shall leave his father and mother and cleave to his wife, and the two shall become one flesh."* [3] Then God called the two people by one name.[4] When a male and female come together, they are no longer two separate people, but they become one and God sees them as one.

After Adam named all the animals, there was found no one suitable for him. So God caused him to sleep, and took from his side one of his ribs, and using that rib God fashioned the woman and brought her to the man.[5]

He took the woman out of man, then brought them together to be one flesh again. Both the male and the female are created in God's image and likeness. In God's eyes both the man and the woman are equally valuable, equally treasured, equally loved. He sees them as one. God calls them "man" and made them male and female. Just as He made lions male and female, and elephants male and female, and every other animal, bird and fish He made male and female, He made man male and female. When God says "man" most of the time He is referring to both the male and the female, to all of mankind.

God created the garden of Eden, prepared everything for man just the way He wanted it with everything man would need, and then placed man in the garden. He gave them dominion over all the works of His Hands, told them to be fruitful and multiply, to subdue the earth. I believe that in heaven we will know the same things that Adam knew in the garden – only better. Remember that God always restores more, not less.

In creation God created the vegetation to reproduce after its kind, He told the animals and the fish and the birds to be fruitful and to multiply after their kind. He told the man and the woman to be fruitful and multiply.[6] There's no evidence in scripture that God ever intended any of that to be temporary, no scripture where God tells it to stop. The present heaven and earth will pass away, but His Word will never pass away,[7] and there is a new heaven and a new earth that will come,[8] a new heaven and a new earth not polluted and perverted by sin.

God told Adam and Eve to have dominion over all the works of His Hands, and Jesus told us that we will rule with Him in the ages to come. [9]

Remember that the word "marriage" refers to a law, a legal contract. Without sin and satan, no law is needed to get man to follow God's ways.

I submit to you that Adam and Eve were never married. There is no record of God conducting a marriage ceremony for Adam and Eve or even referring to marriage concerning them. God's Word was sufficient. There was no one found suitable for Adam. God took one of Adam's ribs, made the woman and brought her to Adam and the two became one flesh again. Done.

They freely walked in God's way, lived life as it was meant to be lived because they knew no other way. Marriage isn't mentioned until well after the fall. When things are as they were intended to be, when they are done God's way as they will be in the resurrection – in Heaven – no law is needed. It's simply done God's way. There is no sin, no temptation to do otherwise, there are no enemies in heaven. All is as it should be.

That's what Jesus meant when He said they will be like the angels in heaven. God's angels are willingly obedient, not tempted with evil. Now there was a time when 1/3 of the angels followed Lucifer in rebellion and were cast out of Heaven. The other 2/3 stayed with God. They do things God's way because that's what they chose. We know of no laws in Heaven to make the angels do things God's way, to make the angels obey God's commands. They are willing servants and messengers of the Most High. He is the Lord of Hosts. They are our servants and ministers because we are God's children.

In Heaven, in the Resurrection, those there are there because they chose to be. They willingly chose to make Jesus their Lord. How much more will a child, an heir, obey and serve the Father than the servants of the kingdom – the angels –obey and serve Him?

This is the power of God – that He has given us the right, the power to become His children.[11] His power, through the cross, the death and the resurrection of His Son, has made us a new creation delivered from the control of the god of this world, made us children, made us heirs. We are no longer slaves of the evil one, but are servants of righteousness. Because we are God's children, everything in us is from Him.[10]   How beautiful!

> *Marriage is a physical example in the earth of Jesus' relationship to His Church*

That is God's power!

God made man male and female, planned us to leave father and mother and become one flesh permanently, to be fruitful and multiply, inseparably one, the husband laying his life down for his wife and loving her as Jesus loves the church, the wife submitting to her husband as she does to the Lord, a place of security, peace, fulfillment, increase and permanent union and oneness. (Ephesians 5:22-25)

One man – one woman – one flesh - for always.

Just as there is one God in three persons – the Father, the Son, and the Holy Spirit – three in One, He intended marriage to be two together as one – two in one. Intimacy, love, commitment, unity.

In the book of Ephesians Paul compares the marriage relationship to Jesus' relationship to His church. And that is exactly why satan has worked so hard, and is still working feverishly, to destroy the relationship between man and woman, and destroy marriage as God intended it to be. It reminds Him of Jesus' relationship to the church. Satan's war is with God and with anything that comes from God, looks like God, acts like God, or reminds him of Jesus.

As we discussed earlier, the entire marriage relationship as planned and purposed by God has gotten completely off track. Through the seduction of the evil one, man has been robbed of the fulfillment and beauty God intended in marriage.

We can see God's love and wisdom in giving u laws concerning marriage – no divorce, no sex outside of marriage, letting each man have his own wife and each woman her own husband[13] - so we wouldn't completely des-troy ourselves.

But destroy ourselves we do – ourselves and our children.

Everywhere we can plainly see, as society moves further and further away from God's plan, the impact of that separation.

We are seeing a massive increase in the destruction and devastation in people's lives and in families everywhere.

But when we change and do it God's way we can avoid the pain, distrust, anger, rage, hurt, and brokenness that is rampant in the earth today.

Now back to your imagination and your ability to dream.

Just like the gift of a man and a woman being one flesh, God gave us our imagination as a gift. And just like marriage, satan has perverted that gift. Our imagination is the ability for us to dream. It is one of His

126

many gifts to us – a tool for Him to communicate with us. And because Jesus has redeemed us and all we are, our imagination, like our marriage, is free to be all He intended it to be. He wants to use our imagination as a canvas where He can paint for us the things He wants to show us, to reveal to us what He has put inside us, to show us all the places He wants to take us.

> *God wants to use our imagination as a canvas where He can paint for us the things He wants to reveal to us*

Because it has been perverted, our imagination has been used for evil rather than for good, used for destruction rather than for blessing and building up, used for man's purposes rather than for God's purposes. It has been given over to the enemy to use rather than submitted to the Father for His use.

In its perversion, the imagination became the birthing ground for all manner of evil plans and schemes, and used by the evil one as a tool to distract God's man from what He had for him.

As a result, we've been warned against dreaming. We've been told that dreaming is a waste of time. Dreamers have often been maligned throughout history.

> *We have been restored to freedom because the cross changed everything*

And in His love, just as He has instructed us about marriage and divorce, God taught us concerning our imaginations. He said whatever is pure, honorable, whatever is of good report, think on these things.[14] From the beginning, like the law of marriage, these instructions were not necessary. Adam walked and talked with God. He was free to decide, think, dream, choose, because there was nothing hindering his relationship with God because, before the fall, everything was from God. Evil had not yet taken over.[15]

Here's the good news!

We have been restored to freedom because the cross changed everything. Everything that separated us from God, everything that was hostile to us, has been removed by the cross. When we make Jesus our Lord, everything is completely new. And all these new things are from God. And now we have the mind of Christ.[16] He wants us to renew our minds to who we are now.

Now that we've been restored to God through the cross of Jesus Christ, He can communicate with us and we can communicate with Him in ways that have not been available for a long time.

We do live in a fallen world, with influences all around us designed to distract us, deceive us, seduce us. But we, because of Jesus, can say what He said, *"the ruler of this world has nothing in me."*[17]

When we renew our minds to who we are now in Christ, we will experience the transformation God wants us to know.[18] When we renew our minds to the fact that God loves us, when our focus becomes His love for us and not on us trying to love Him and trying to find ways to serve Him and please Him, not only our minds but our lives will be transformed into a freedom we've never before known.

With that freedom comes the freedom to dream, to imagine, because we will be dreaming God's possibilities. Unlike in the past when we were told that our imagination was a tool for evil and day dreaming was a waste of time, we can now experience the wonder and joy of the Father's heart and mind for us. We can dream dreams together with the God Who created us. Our imagination comes alive with His life. We discover a whole new dimension that was previously dormant, blocked off from us.

> *You are on the shoreline*
> *of the vast limitlessness*
> *that God wants*
> *to reveal to you*

So then, dreaming is good. Imagination is a wonderful gift from our Father so we can be bigger on the inside than we are on the outside. Your imagination and the dreams He gives you are a key to your destiny. Your passions are a key to what He has gifted you to do and what He's given you to accomplish.

And it is God's heart for each one of us that we be transformed by renewing our minds so we can live freely in the fullness Jesus died to provide for us, to know and live out the destiny that He is waiting to reveal to us.

If you have the ability to accomplish your dream, you aren't dreaming God's dream for you. If you have the ability to accomplish the dream you have, you are short–changing yourself. You are settling for less than what is possible for you.

When you have a dream that is impossible, you have stepped up to the starting gate. You are on the shoreline of the vast limitlessness that God wants to reveal to you. You are just beginning to tap into what God wants to do in your life. You are standing at the beginning of a very exciting journey. *"God is able to do far more abundantly beyond all that we ask or think, according to the power that works within us."* (Ephesians 3:20)   When you hook up with God it is impossible for anything to be impossible.

Because with God all things are possible!

It's your choice –

You can reach the fast food store at the end of the street, or the farthest star in the universe, or the farthest star in the farthest universe that we haven't even discovered yet.

How big is your dream? Let God give you His dream and show you all that is out there. The Hubble telescope isn't making galaxies as it goes. It is merely finding what is already there. You have big dreams. You have a bigger God. God is bigger than the dream He gave you.

Take that step out of the boat. Out of the ordinary. Out of this world. Discover your destiny.

Your time is now.

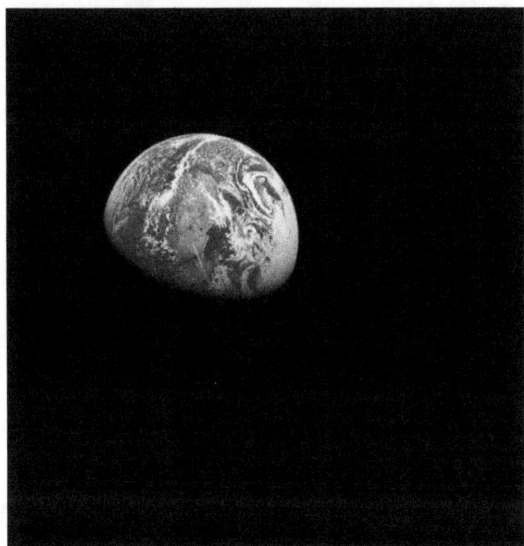

You are equipped with gifts,
talents, ideas, and dreams that
the world you are in needs

CHAPTER SEVEN

INTENTIONALLY UNIQUE
NO ONE CAN BE THE YOU
YOU WERE CREATED TO BE

ALL OF US, AT ONE TIME OR ANOTHER, spend our energies trying to be what we are not, trying to be what we think we are supposed to be. Perhaps more often we live our lives either trying to be what others expect us to be or what they have told us we are.

We spend way too much time trying to be what we are not.

Everybody needs to be loved. Often our efforts to be what others want us to be are rooted in that need. We think that others will love us if we were just somehow what they want us to be. Another reason – and perhaps the main reason – is that we don't much like ourselves. We find it difficult, if not impossible, to love ourselves. So we try to change who and what we are, thinking that in so doing we will at last be fulfilled, happy, content, and finally able to be loved. We go to motivational speakers, learn mind–changing techniques, repeat a list of mantras, meditate, all in an effort to change the things in us that we have decided are not right or that others have told us need to change. And the burden is on us to perform and jump through all the right hoops, to remember everything we're supposed to say and everything we're supposed to do and when to say it and when to do it. The burden is on us to change. It's a huge, heavy load we carry.

We end up exhausted, worn out, empty, frustrated. And back where we started.

And still not loved the way we need or want to be. It becomes a vicious cycle that we find difficult to break, always looking for the right solution, the right program, the right combination of steps to take, the right formula to follow.

Whew!

Now, it's true that we're all a little messed up. Remember the whole fall in the garden thing and how we have all been born into that sin, that death, that separation from Life and Love?

What we all deal with in our own way is the fact that we were not designed to be separated from Life, separated from Love. We were designed to be one with Love. We were designed for dominion. We were designed to reign in life. Our insides know that. Our spirit knows there's more. We all have a "knowing" inside us that tells us that there is something greater, something more.[1]

That is why, when you study civilizations from all over the world throughout history, you'll find there has always been some form of worship of a god or gods, some form of religion, some establishment of right and wrong governing the community, a knowledge of a greater power.

> *God has put within each one of us the knowledge of Himself*

Why? Where did that come from?

There was no one going from tribe to tribe teaching these things to each people group. Yet we find everywhere certain universal beliefs, certain universal rights and wrongs that they live by. For instance, it is never right to run in the face of battle, it is never right to break a covenant, it is never right to commit murder.

You see, God has put within each one of us the knowledge of Himself. But because of the fall, man no longer had that direct connection. He denied the existence of God, resisted God, and did everything he could to remove God from his society, even to imprison and execute those who chose to worship Him. And since man chose not to honor Him as God, their hearts became darkened.[2]

Even though their hearts were darkened that desire to know God, to be loved, and the desire for dominion remained. And because man chose not to honor God, he was left to his own devices to fill that need. And satan was there every step of the way to direct him as far away from God as possible.

And, apart from God, that need for love continues unfulfilled. There are brief, passing experiences of contentment and exhilaration, but the emptiness remains. Fulfillment never comes. And even when we get born again and are once again united to that Life that we

IMAGINE THE POSSIBILITIES

were denied, we often still feel an emptiness and frustration because we are told that we now need to focus on what we need to do to please God. We are told that if we just love God enough and serve Him enough we'll be blessed, He'll answer our prayers, everything will be alright, but we always feel we are falling short. We always feel we are falling short

- because we are.

We're still looking in the wrong direction.

Jesus told us the greatest commandment is to love the Lord your God with all your heart, all your soul, all your mind.[3] Jesus made that statement while the Old Covenant was still in effect. The generation He spoke to was still under the law. No one has ever been able to fully obey the law except Jesus. He alone fulfilled the law. We may desperately want to, we may earnestly try to, but every one of us falls short. Throughout history man has fallen short. No one can keep the law perfectly. Constantly.

But, then, the law was not given for us to keep. It was given to show us our need for a Savior.[4] When He preached, Jesus said, *"Repent for the kingdom of Heaven is at hand."*

Matthew 4:17

The word "repent" means to change your mind. Jesus was telling the people that it was time to change their way of thinking because the kingdom of Heaven was about to come. He introduced them to a whole new way of thinking about their relationship with God. At the beginning of His earthly ministry He went to the synagogue, and, as was His custom, He stood up and read a verse from the prophet Isaiah and began to say,

"Today this scripture has been fulfilled in your hearing."

Luke 4:16-21

Notice it says, *"He began to say."* That wasn't all He said. He had much more to say after that. He was teaching the people that everything was about to change. That was the "good news" that He preached everywhere He went.

"The Spirit of the Lord is upon Me, because the Lord has anointed Me to preach the gospel to the poor. He has sent Me to proclaim release to the captives, and recovery of sight to the blind, to set free those who are downtrodden, to proclaim the favorable year of the Lord."

Luke 4:18-19

"The Spirit of the Lord Yahweh is upon Me, because the Lord has anointed Me to bring good news to the afflicted; He has sent Me to bind up the brokenhearted, to proclaim liberty to the captives, and freedom to prisoners; to proclaim the favorable year of the Lord, and the day of vengeance of our God; to comfort all who mourn, to grant those who mourn in Zion,

giving them a garland instead of ashes, the oil of gladness instead of mourning, the mantle of praise instead of a spirit of fainting. So they will be called the oaks of righteousness, the planting of the Lord, that He may be glorified."

Isaiah 61:1-3

Jesus also said, *"Come to Me, all who are weary and heavy laden, and I will give you rest."* Matthew 11:28

Rest from trying to fulfill the law.

Jesus said that the greatest and foremost commandment is, *"You shall love the Lord your God with all your heart and with all your soul and will all your mind."*

Matthew 22:37-38

And we know that no one but Jesus has ever been able to perfectly fulfill the law. The truth is that God never intended us to focus on our love for Him. And the reason for that is simple. He knows that, in ourselves, we can't love Him perfectly. Everything He does He does because of His love for us and because of what Jesus did for us, not in response to our love for Him or our service to Him.

> *When we turn our face to Him and receive the fullness of His love for us, like a flower soaking up the warmth of the sun and the refreshing rain, everything changes*

The scriptures teach us that we love because He first loved us.[5] He loves us first, then we can love. He sent His Son to die in our place because of His love for us. He extends His grace to us out of His love for us. And He wants us to receive His grace and everything His grace supplies because of His love for us. Jesus Himself said that He came not to be served, but to serve.[6] How awesome it is to stop and consider that!

Jesus came to serve!

We've had things kind of backward. Even as born again believers our focus has been on what we need to do to please God and how to get Him to bless us and answer our prayers. We focus on keeping a law we were never intended to or able to keep, trying to love God in a way we were never able to, when what He wants is for us to receive what He came to do for us, what He's already done for us. The Holy Spirit records in the book of Hebrews that we are to be diligent to enter His rest. The entire 4th chapter of Hebrews is all about resting in what Jesus has done. He wants our focus to be on how much He loves us. *"For God so loved the world that He gave His only begotten Son."* He didn't just love us, He loved us *so much* that He gave us His Son.[7]

See also 1 Peter 4:11 - we are to act out of that which He has supplied.

When we get our eyes off ourselves and simply turn our face to Him and receive the fullness of His love for us, like a flower soaking up the warmth of the sun and the refreshing rain, everything changes. We stop being afraid of who we are.

When you focus on His love for you, you will notice three things happen:

-   Your love for Him will grow beyond limits you once thought impossible to reach.

-   Out of that love, you find that you love yourself.

All the self hate has somehow vanished.

And your whole life has completely changed.

You are now living out of the flow of the energy of His love instead of out of your own energy, your own inspiration, your own determination.

You are now living your life out of the flow of an energy and power that never changes, never leaves, never weakens, never ends. His love for you is constant, eternal and perfect.

> *Your day is sprinkled with love notes from your Father*

When you focus on how much He loves you, you find you don't need to keep reminding yourself what you need to do, what you need to remember. You don't need to keep repeating mantras to re-energize or find some way to look inside, to "dig down deeper" when you are feeling weak or overwhelmed.

Instead, your day is sprinkled with love notes from your Father. You will continue to grow in awareness of all the things that He does every day – just for you.

When you see His smile, when you hear His laugh, you turn your face to Him again and receive.

> *You no longer strive to be loved because you already are*

Simply receive.

And it starts all over again.

It just keeps getting better.

- The third thing you notice is that you find yourself loving those around you.

Without even trying.

All the love you are swimming in is splashing over onto them.

You no longer have to prove yourself.

To yourself or to anyone else.

And they no longer have to prove themselves to you to earn your love. You love them just the way they are. Right where they're at. You can't help it. You no longer strive to be loved because you already are. You no longer have to work to love others because you see in them the beauty your Father created in them. You are living in a love that is impossible to describe, impossible to contain, impossible to deny.

It seems "too good to be true" – but then all that beauty and wonder originates with Him.

Because, well, that's Who He is.

God is love. In that love, and out of that love, let God show you who you really are.

Lift up your eyes, see beyond where you are today, look toward all the beautiful, exciting tomorrows that are out there just waiting for you to discover.

Just waiting for you to be you.

> *Only you can bring tears of joy to your Father's eyes as He watches you be all He created you to be*

Imagine the possibilities.

Living life totally joyful – 100% committed to being the you God created you to be.

Because only you can be the you *you* were created to be.

Only you can blossom into the you *you* are to become. Only you can fulfill your destiny.

Only you can bring tears of joy to your Father's eyes as He watches you be all He created you to be.

Tears of joy because you are looking to Him, trusting Him,

Walking with Him,

Talking with Him,

Having conversations with Him.

Tears of joy because He gets to lavish His love on you, because you have stopped trying to earn it.

One with Him.

Moment by moment.

Step by step.

Breath by breath.

That's what He created you for.

To be one with Him.

His Image.

His likeness.

To experience His possibilities.

And with Him, nothing is impossible.

His Word says "with" God nothing is impossible. It does not say "for" God nothing is impossible. Of course nothing is impossible for God. But He specifically said, "with" God nothing is impossible. "With" Him is the key.

You are born again. You are one with Him. He is in you, you are in Him. You are *with* Him, and *with* Him nothing shall be impossible. You can do all He's given you to do. Jesus is the reason.

> *Are you beginning to realize just how special you are?*

No one else can do what you can do. No one else can do it the way you can do it.

Because there is no one else like you. There has never been anyone else like you. There will never be anyone else like you. Ever.

Your fingerprints have never been nor will ever be anyone else's fingerprints.

Your DNA has never been nor will ever be anyone else's DNA. Your specific combination of gifts, talents, abilities and dreams are uniquely you. No one else has that same combination, in the same proportions, the same way. Your dreams and passions are keys to what you are destined for.

Only you can accomplish what you can do.

Are you beginning to realize just how special you are?

God created you. If you are born again, He is your Father. He has given you His kingdom.

<u>HIS</u> kingdom.

His <u>KINGDOM</u>.

His ETERNAL KINGDOM.

God created you and everything you see, and everything you haven't seen yet.

And did you know that He hasn't stopped creating?

He has finished His work. He has done everything. But His word is still working, creating.

Science has discovered that the universe is still expanding. The Bible tells us why.

The Bible tells us that God's Word is light and that God spoke everything into existence. He created the heavens and the earth with His words. He created everything with light. God said "Light be, and light was."[8] God never told the light to stop. The light is still going. And going. And going.

Space is measured in light years. The speed of light is 186,000 miles a second, 700 million miles an hour.

There are stars that we are just now seeing that burned out a long time ago. They quit giving light long before their light reached us. That's how far away they are. It's hard to get our minds around that. You might find it interesting to remember the next time you are looking at a beautiful sunrise that the sunrise actually occurred 8 minutes earlier. It takes that long for the light to reach Earth! And the sun is much closer to Earth than millions of other stars that we can see and those we are still discovering.

186,000 miles per second. 700 million miles an hour.

Quantum physics has shown that the common element in all matter is light! The common element in all matter is God's Word. Science – specifically quantum physics – has discovered that all matter in its most basic form, at the smallest level, can be measured and studied in terms of – you guessed it –

IMAGINE THE POSSIBILITIES

light. Quantum physics tells us that subatomic particles are not made of energy – they are energy. A Swiss physicist named S. Bell provided mathematical proof of the common connection of all matter in terms of light behaving as a wave. Our bodies are made of light and maintain the characteristics of light. The Nobel Prize winning physicist David Bohm has written that light is both the medium and the message of the information in the universe. He has written about what he calls the "implicate order of the light picture of the universe." His concept suggests that the entire universe is an ever–changing cosmic picture of light that is layered with information.

According to new scientific thought, all matter consists of forms of light. Even in its smallest state, nothing is still. A quantum physicist would say that light in this context does not on its own slow down – it always moves at the speed of light. It can be made to slow down, but it can never be stopped. It is always moving. That's why we can speak to our bodies and command them to be healed and see them healed. That's why we can speak to mountains to be removed and trees to wither and they will obey us. God's Word is light and when we speak God's Word in Jesus' Name we are speaking forth light. Light speaking to light. When we speak light with Jesus' authority, the One through whom all things were created and by Whom all things exist, the light we are speaking to must obey.

"For by Him all things were created, both in the heavens and on earth, visible and invisible, whether thrones or dominions or rulers or authorities – all things have been created through Him and for Him."

Col 1:16

"Yet for us there is but one God, the Father, from Whom are all things and we exist for

Him; and one Lord Jesus Christ, by Whom are all things, and we exist through Him."

1 Cor 8:6

"In the beginning was the Word, and the Word was with God, and the Word was God. He was in the beginning with God. All things came into being through Him, and apart from Him nothing came into being that has come into being. In Him was life, and the life was the Light of men. ...and the Word became flesh and dwelt among us."

John 1:1-4, 14

That's how Jesus calmed the wind and the waves and turned the water into wine. That is how He raised the dead, healed the sick, cleansed the lepers. The Author of light spoke to light. That is why He gave us His Name and told us to go do the same.

Not all light is directly visible to our eyes. Gamma-rays, ultraviolet light, infrared light,

X-rays – all these are some of the ways we refer to light. But they are all light. There are no breaks or boundaries in the light spectrum. It is a continuous wave of energy, flowing from visible to invisible.

Wow! God said, "Light be. And light was." And it still is. 186,000 miles per second. 700 million miles per hour. And Jesus has called us to reign with Him – in life now and in the ages to come!

Wow!

And God knows all the stars by name. He even knows how many there are![9] The black holes in space aren't mysteries to Him – He knows what's on the other side.

So – let go of who others want you to be. Let go of who *you* think you should be. Turn your whole face to your Father Who made you and let Him show you who you really are. There's a whole lot out there for you, there are worlds for you to discover, a destiny for you to fulfill.

There is so much more than you ever imagined.

"Call to Me and I will answer you, and I will tell you great and mighty things, which you do not know."

Jeremiah 33:3

"Thus says the Lord, 'Stand by the ways and see and ask for the ancient paths, where the good way is, and walk in it; and you will find rest for your souls.'"   Jeremiah 6:16

Receive. God is proud of you.

Dream. Your possibilities are as limitless as God Himself.

You are intentionally unique.

So is your destiny.

Your time is now.

The world needs who you are

CHAPTER EIGHT

WHAT YOU NEVER KNEW ABOUT CHRISTOPHER COLUMBUS

TAKING A FRESH LOOK

HE ACCOMPLISHED WHAT NO ONE before him had ever done, or thought was possible.

Sound familiar?

What he did required courage, persistence, faith.

Also sound familiar?

He accomplished what he did because he was given a dream by God.

From Columbus' own writings we read:

"At a very early age I began to sail upon the ocean. For more than forty years,

I have sailed everywhere that people go."

He spent most of his early life doing what had always been done. But then we read –

"I prayed to the most merciful Lord about my heart's great desire, and He gave me the spirit and intelligence for the task: seafaring, astronomy, geometry, arithmetic, skill in drafting spherical maps and placing correctly the cities, rivers, mountains and ports. I also studied cosmology, history, chronology, and philosophy.

"It was the Lord Who put into my mind (I could feel His hand upon me) the fact that it would be possible to sail from here to the Indies. All who heard my project rejected it with laughter, ridiculing me.

"There is no question that the inspiration was from the Holy Spirit, because He comforted me with rays of marvelous illumination from the Holy Scriptures ...

encouraging me continually to press forward and without ceasing for a moment they now encourage me to make haste.

"Our Lord Jesus desired to perform a very obvious miracle in the voyage to the Indies, to comfort me and the whole people of God. I spent seven years in the royal court, discussing the matter with many persons of great reputation and wisdom in all the arts; and in the end they concluded that it was all foolishness, so they gave it up.

"But since things generally come to pass that were predicted by our Savior Jesus Christ, we should also believe that this particular prophesy will come to pass. Jesus said that all things would pass away but not His marvelous Word.

"I said that I would state my reason: I hold alone to the sacred and Holy Scriptures, and to the interpretations of prophecy given by certain devout persons.

"It is possible that those who see this book will accuse me of being unlearned in literature, of being a layman and a sailor. I reply with the words of Matt. 11:25: 'Lord because Thou hast hid these things from the wise and prudent, and hath revealed them to babes.'

"I am a most unworthy sinner, but I have cried out to the Lord for grace and mercy, and they have covered me completely. I have found the sweetest consolations since I made it my whole purpose to enjoy His marvelous presence.

"For the execution of the journey to the Indies I did not make use of intelligence, mathematics or maps. It is simply the fulfillment of what Isaiah had prophesied. All this is what I desire to write down for you in this book.

"No one should ever fear to undertake any task in the Name of our Savior, if it is just and if the intention is purely for His Holy service.

The working out of all things has been assigned to each person by our Lord, but it all happens according to His sovereign will even though He gives advice.

"He lacks nothing that it is in the power of men to give him. Oh what a gracious Lord, Who desires that people should perform for Him those things for which He holds Himself responsible!

"I said that some prophecies remained yet to be fulfilled. These are great and wonderful things for the earth, and the signs are that the Lord is hastening the end. The fact that the gospel must still be preached to so many lands in such a short time, this is what convinces me."[1]

The fact that the Bible played a great part in Columbus' actions, thoughts and decisions is evident from his writings. His concept of sailing to the Indies was not so much the result of geographical theories, but was birthed out of his faith in what the Bible had to say, most prominently, the book of Isaiah.

From his "Book of Prophecies" Columbus cited the following passages from Scripture:

Ps 97:1

> *The Lord reigns, let the earth rejoice;*
> *let the many islands be glad.*

Isa 42:10

> *Sing to the Lord a new song, sing His*
> *praise from the end of the earth!*
>
> *You who go down to the sea, and all*
> *that is in it. You islands, and those who*
> *dwell on them.*

Is 49:1

> *Listen to Me, O islands, and pay*
> *attention, you peoples from afar. The*
> *Lord called me from the womb; from*
> *the body of my mother He named me.*

Is 49:6

> *He says, "It is too small a thing that You should be My Servant to raise up the tribes of Jacob and to restore the preserved ones of Israel; I will also make You a light of the nations so that My salvation may reach to the end of the earth."*

Is 51:5

> *My righteousness is near, My salvation has gone forth, And My arms will judge the peoples; The coastlands will wait for Me, and for My arm they will wait expectantly.*

Is 60:9

> *Surely the coastlands will wait for Me; and the ships of Tarshish will come first, to bring your sons from afar, their silver and their gold with them, for the name of the Lord your God, and for the*

> *Holy One of Israel because He has glorified you.*

Is 65:1

> *I permitted Myself to be sought by those who did not ask for Me; I permitted Myself to be found by those who did not seek Me. I said, 'Here am I, here am I,' to a nation which did not call on My name.*

Mt 28:19

> *Go therefore and make disciples of all the nations, baptizing them in the name of the Father and the Son and the Holy Spirit*

Acts 1:8

> *But you will receive power when the Holy Spirit has come upon you; and you shall be My witnesses both in Jerusalem,*

and in all Judea and Samaria, and even
to the remotest part of the earth.

Can you see his vision – his dream?

His dream came from God, but he didn't have an easy time. People opposed him. The pieces did not just fall together. He didn't all at once find open doors and willing hands to assist him. He spent seven years convincing the monarchs of Europe to finance his expedition. He was forced to endure the *"ridicule of the wise and learned of his day."*

But remember Jesus said *"In the world you have tribulation, but take courage; I have overcome the world"*[2]

He persevered because he had a dream from God. He had prayed to God concerning his dream, and the Lord blessed him with the intelligence and the *"spirit for the task."*

He held on to the dream.

He knew what God had given him to do.

He was finally able to convince Queen Isabella and King Ferdinand to finance his expedition. The queen's commission to him included:

"It is hoped that by God's assistance some of the continents and islands in the ocean will be discovered... for the glory of God."[1]

At last he and his crew set sail on August 3, 1492. The day they set sail every crew member, including Columbus, received Holy Communion, and *"in the Name of Jesus ordered the sails to be set and left the harbor"* for the open sea.

The first island they landed on Columbus named San Salvador, which means "Holy Savior." On each island they landed he had his men erect a cross *"as a token of Jesus Christ our Lord and in honor of the Christian faith."* [1]

He set out on a journey that no one had ever taken to go where no one had ever gone and that most thought was foolish and doomed to fail. Three months later, he discovered a whole new world.

He made a total of four voyages to that new world.

It wasn't easy. There were many hard times. He was opposed. Many tried to talk him out of it, many tried to stop him.

But because he believed what had been given him by the Lord, he discovered the new world.

According to his personal log, he viewed himself as a *"servant of the Most High Savior Jesus Christ,"* and his purpose in seeking undiscovered lands was to *"bring the gospel of Jesus Christ to the heathens, and to bring the Word of God to unknown coastlands."*[1]

Which was the same reason the king and queen financed his voyage. And it was the same reason the pilgrims set out from Holland for that same new world. They wanted to find a place where they could freely worship God, and to bring the gospel of Jesus Christ to the inhabitants of that land. Because of the large wooden crosses that Columbus had erected, and the prayers he prayed over each place he landed, they were drawn in that same Spirit to worship God there and bring the gospel of Jesus Christ to the people there. They continued what he started.

Christopher Columbus didn't create the new world. He wasn't the first person to set foot on the lands he discovered. He knew that others were already there because of what he read in the scriptures. The people that were already there were the reason he went. He discovered what was already there and because he did millions after him have been able to benefit from what he had the courage to do.

Sound familiar?

Dream.

Trust.

Persevere.

Imagine the possibilities.

Your time is now.

Discover your God~given

passion

Fulfill your God~given

destiny

CHAPTER NINE

PROGRESSIONS

*MONUMENTS OF MAN'S
ACCOMPLISHMENTS*

MAN USED FIRE.

Then he discovered electricity.

He experienced the first sound over a wire.

All the way to the next room.

Then he had phones the size of a credit card that could be used to talk to someone on the other side of the world.

Man had horses.

Then he had trains.

Then cars.

Planes.

Jets.

The Concord.

He had key punch.

Then computers that filled several rooms.

Then he had computers the size of a grain of rice.

Man spent centuries looking at the moon and dreaming.

Then he walked on the moon.

He made eyeglasses that made things bigger so he could see better.

Then he had binoculars.

And telescopes.

Then he discovered there were other planets besides Earth.

He discovered there was a whole solar system.

Then he had Hubble, and discovered there were whole galaxies beyond his own – and bigger ones.

And more galaxies were still being created.

He launched a missile.

Then he launched a manned missile.

Then he went around the earth a few times.

Then he went around the earth for many days.

Then he went to the moon.

And walked there.

Then he had a space station that he could go to and come back from and go back to again. And live there.

Did you know that all these things were possible for man to do from the foundation of the earth? When we did them wasn't when they were created. The possibility for us to do all these things has always been here. We just didn't know how. Once we discovered the principles that governed them, we were able to do them.

For instance, the laws of aerodynamics that make it possible for planes to fly were in existence from the time God created the earth. It just took us time to discover them, and to learn how to use them to our advantage.

> *When you combine the you that you are created to be with this time in the earth's history, only God knows the wonderful things that are about to happen*

Using the physical laws that God put in place we came up with inventions, each one building on the knowledge gained from the previous one. We put our discoveries together and came up with even more wonderful discoveries.

We discovered what had always been there.

With only six to ten percent.

You may have heard it said that you're not here by accident.

But have you really stopped to think about it? It's true. Your time on this earth has a purpose. Your arrival here at this specific time in history is not an accident. You have been given gifts, talents, and desires that God intends to use to bring about things that have never been done before, have never been discovered before, have never been tried before, to be done at this specific time in history.

You have been put together on purpose. You were created to have a significant impact on this world in your generation.

Will you impact

     an individual?

     a city?

     a nation?

Will you go where no one has yet gone?

Will you discover what has yet to be known?

Will you try what has never been tried?

The you that you are – your fingerprints, your DNA, your gifts, passions, talents, dreams – have arrived here at this point in history, with all the available science, technology, discoveries, and inventions, on purpose. When you combine the you that you are created to be with this time in the earth's history, only God knows the wonderful things that are about to happen. And right now, He is the only One Who knows. And He's waiting to show it all to you.

Go ahead.

Your time is now.

Your will power will eventually

fail you ~

God's power will never fail you

CHAPTER TEN

THE CITY LIGHTS AND THE COUNTRY STARS

LEARNING A GREAT LESSON

WHEN YOU GET A NEW piece of electronic equipment and you want to know the right way to use it, to get the most out of it and use all of its great features and gadgets, you read the owner's manual. When you run into problems, you call the toll free number printed in the manual and talk to the manufacturer himself. You get the problem solved, and the equipment works perfectly, bringing you the enjoyment from all the bells and whistles that make it so great.

Well, did you know that the same is true of you, your life?

More so.

How much greater are you than a PC, a DVR or a flat screen TV? How different would your life be if you had access to the manufacturer of your life, the One Who designed you and put you together?

What if you could go to Him when something wasn't working right, and He would show you how to fix it?

What if you could go to Him and He would show you all the characteristics of your life, all the "bells and whistles" that make you so great, and teach you how your life is supposed to work so you can get the full benefit of all the "features" He created you with?

What if you could be in a place where you could clearly see all the things you just know are there but are somehow blocked from your view? You know, that "something" that you can't quite find the right words for, can't quite get your hands on?

How different would your life be?

When you are in the city at night and look up to the sky, you don't see many stars. But if you get in your car and drive to the country that same night you see thousands of bright, beautiful stars.

Why? What's the difference between the city and the country?

Are the stars only in the country and not in the city? Someone who has never been out of the city or who has never been taught about the stars might possibly come to that conclusion. They may not know that there are more than the few stars they see each night.

But, of course, we know that the stars are everywhere. They were always there. They were there when you were downtown. You just couldn't see them from where you were at that time. The problem wasn't with the stars, but with your vantage point. The place where you were standing was the reason you couldn't see the stars.

> *God has always had a plan and a destiny for you*

What happens is that the man–made lights in the city block out the God–made light of the stars. Even though the light of the stars is infinitely greater than the man–made lights, man's lights still have the ability to block out the light of the stars. Out in the country, where there are no man–made lights, thousands of beautiful stars are visible.

The stars didn't just appear when you got to the country, they were always there. You just couldn't see them when you were under man's lights.

We can learn a great lesson from the city lights and the country stars.

> *When we get out from under the perceived limitations imposed on us by man and step into the limitlessness of God Himself, we will see far beyond anything we ever thought possible*

There are as many stars over the city as there are in the country. When you put yourself in the right situation, you can see what has always been there. When you put yourself in the right situation, you can see what God has always had there for you. Man–made doctrines and theologies that shape our belief systems have the ability to block out the God–made truths that reveal His reality to us. God has always had a plan and a destiny for you. You just may not have been able to see it because of where you have been standing.

Just as the man–made lights block out the greater lights that exist, so also our own devices, our own plans and ideas, man's theories and philosophies, politics, religion and doctrines can block out the greater light of God's plans, purposes, truth and ways of doing things.

When we get out from under the influence of our own ideas and endeavors, out from under man's traditions and doctrines, we can see with more clarity what God has always had right there for us to experience. When we get out from under the perceived limitations imposed on us by man and step into the limitlessness of God Himself, we will see far beyond anything we ever thought possible. We begin to see our lives change, promises come to pass, prayers answered – a whole new world of "what's always been there" for us.

The galaxies that Hubble is discovering have always been there. It wasn't until we knew how to get there and how to photograph them that we could see them and learn about them.

But God wasn't surprised. He always knew they were there. And He even knows what's beyond those.

He made them.

He knows each of those stars by name.[1]

He knows your name. He knows how many hairs are on your head.

> *His light is there to illuminate all the dark places that are now confusing, overwhelming and frightening*

If you have the courage, He will show you things and take you places that would blow your mind if you knew them now.

The One that created your brain, that gave you your gifts and talents and dreams, your DNA and your fingerprints, is right there, with you, in you, to lead you into all that you don't even know yet.

He has come in to dine with you, which is to say He is with you and shares all your moments, talks with you, and opens up to you all that is in His heart concerning you. It is His good pleasure to give you the kingdom, and He delights in showing it all to you. He is there to show you how your life is supposed to work.

His light is there to illuminate all the dark places that are now confusing, overwhelming, and frightening.

You know, like when you walk into a room at night when all the lights are off and it is pitch black – where you can't see your hand when you hold it in front of your face – you are unsure of exactly where you are, unsure of where to step, where to turn. Even if it's a room you are in every day, when there is no light you are not sure how to find that thing that you came into the room to get without stubbing your toe.

But, when you turn on a light, even if it's only a little match, the uncertainty vanishes. You know exactly where you are and where to go. Even a small amount of light will show you how to get to where you want to go without knocking over the lamp.

God will turn on lights for you and show you exactly where to step.

If you have never been out of the city and you have never been told that the stars are out there, you would never know what you have been missing.

Those of us who have been to the country know about all the bright, beautiful stars, the shooting stars, and all the wonders in the night sky. It's hard to find the right words to accurately describe it. Those who have never been out of the city are unaware of all that beauty.

In the same way, if you have never been told how much God loves you, how much He cares about you, how much He has prepared for you, to show you, the gifts He has for you, you would not know what you have been missing.

Those of us who have left the "city" – have left the interference of the man–made theologies and doctrines, and have taken that journey to the "country" – into God's reality and truth, have tasted His beauty and the wonders of all He has done. We have taken a peek into all the splendor and limitlessness that is our God. It's hard to find the right words to describe it.

If you are hungry for Him, He will reveal His heart to you. *"Blessed are those who hunger and thirst for righteousness, for they shall be satisfied."*

Matthew 5:6

He said, *"You will seek Me and find Me, when you search for Me with all your heart."*

Jeremiah 29:13

So get out from under all the man–made ideas, traditions, doctrines, philosophies and mindsets.

Look up and see what has always been there for you. Walk in His light. Call on the Manufacturer. He'll fix what's broken in your life.

IMAGINE THE POSSIBILITIES

Reach.

Stretch.

It's your time.

You will never know what can

happen until you step

out of the boat

CHAPTER ELEVEN

THE BEGINNING
HEARING GOD'S VOICE

THE LAST CHAPTER of this book is the beginning of a whole new journey for you, a whole new beginning of all that awaits you in God. Put your hand in His, step out of the boat, and take that exciting journey of discovering all that He has prepared and reserved for you.

How hard is it to hear God's voice?

Not hard at all.

Jesus said , *"My sheep know my voice."*[1]

If you are born again, you belong to Him. In the same way that you earnestly desire to communicate with your children, to teach them all the things they do not yet know, God, too, wants to communicate with you.

Remember, He is the One Who made you and knows how you work. He has made you able to hear Him and communicate with Him.

> *You are equipped with gifts, talents, ideas, and dreams that the world you are in needs*

When you were born again, the communication that was once broken between you and God was restored. You now have the ability to hear His voice, to walk and talk with Him just as Adam once did. Just as God taught Adam about the world He made for him and had placed him in, He wants to teach you about the world He has placed you in.

Don't forget that it is not an accident that you were born and are here now. Your loving heavenly Father has equipped you with gifts, talents, ideas, and dreams that the world you are in needs. You are timed to be here at this season in Earth's history to combine your gifts, talents, ideas and dreams with the technology and the knowledge that is now available, and to go into all the new places that man has not yet seen and discover what man has not yet discovered. There is someone alive right now, or will be alive in your lifetime, that needs who you are.

Your God–given dreams are intentionally bigger than you. They are intentionally bigger than what has ever been done before. They are intentionally not what everyone else is doing. They are intentionally not the way everyone else is doing it. They all intentionally require courage because they will take you where you have never been before and have you doing what you have never done before. But on the other side of that courage is Jesus lovingly waiting for you to take His hand and run with Him into all the beauty of all you do not yet know.

> *Don't be afraid to dream your dream*

The result of that journey is the most exciting and fulfilling life imaginable.

What could you do if you weren't limited to what you can do?

What could you do if you weren't limited to what others say about what you can do?

What could you do if you weren't limited to man's philosophy, man's ideas, man's way of doing things?

What could you do if your only limits were God Himself – Who, by the way, is limitless?

What could you discover?

What could you achieve?

Where will you leave your footprint?

How far will you reach into the unknown?

How far will you reach into the hearts and lives of the ones you love, and the strangers you meet every day?

Where will you be next year if you started your journey today?

What opportunities and dreams are exclusively yours?

No one else can do what you can do. No one else can do it the way you can do it.

So don't be afraid to dream your dream. Don't be afraid to reach beyond where you are now. You never know the beauty that awaits you.

With your hand in Jesus' hand, you will not go wrong. When you fall, He will lift you up.

Remember when Peter walked on the water? The Bible says he began to sink. How fast do you sink when you step into water? Pretty fast. But it says he BEGAN to sink. And Jesus was right there to keep Him from sinking completely into the water.

"But seeing the wind, he became frightened, and beginning to sink he cried out, 'Lord, save me!' Immediately Jesus stretched out His hand and took hold of Him, and said to Him, 'You of little faith, why did you doubt?' When they got into the boat, the wind stopped. And those who were in the boat worshipped Him, saying, 'You are certainly God's Son!' "   Matthew 14:30-33

When you take a wrong step, He will lovingly lead you back to the right path.

When you can't see the way to go, Jesus will turn on the light for you. When you feel like you've gone as far as it is possible to go, He will lift the veil and show you more.

When you feel uncertain, He will assure you.

When you feel like you have to walk on water to get where you are going you will find out that, with Jesus, you have been walking on water all along and didn't even know it.

He made it so easy.

When the hard times come, He will show you how to use the power and authority He has given you to overcome anything that satan brings against you.

> *What waits for you will take your breath away*

Jesus has already defeated every enemy, and there is nothing that your enemy can bring against you that will succeed.[2]

Your enemy will surely try to stop you. But because of what Jesus has done for you your enemy will not triumph. You will. Jesus will show you how.

Take that step.

Start your journey.

What waits for you will take your breath away.

Where will you leave your footprint?

On another world?

On someone else's heart who will one day leave their footprint on another world?

Learn the lesson from the city lights and the country stars.

Step out of the boat.

Look up.

Will you be the one who launches out into the
beauty of the future prepared for you by
your loving Heavenly Father?

Or will you be one of those who stand watching as someone else lifts off into the great unknown?

Imagine the possibilities

Fulfill your destiny

Your time is now

Peter said, "Lord, if it's You,

bid me to

come to You on the water."

Jesus said,

"Come."

REFERENCES

Introduction

1. Jeremiah 29:11, Psalm 139
2. Genesis 1:26
3. Psalm 91:11-12
4. Jeremiah 29:11
5. Zephaniah 3:17, Is 62:5

Chapter 2
6 – 10 %

1. Information from Mensa International
2. Isaiah 49:16, Zechariah 2:8
3. Song of Solomon 2:8
4. Luke 12:32

Chapter 3
A Whole New Life

1. Romans 5:14,15,19
2. Genesis 11:1-9
3. Isaiah 14:12-15, Ezekiel 28:12-18, John 10:10
4. 2 Corinthians 5:17-18
5. John 10:4-5, 14-15, 14:16-17, 26, 16:13-15, I Corinthians 2:16
6. John 16:15

Chapter 4
Moving Forward

1. Philippians 2:13
2. John 14:1
3. John 14:27
4. Colossians 3:15
5. Rom 8:1, 38-39
6. James 1:5
7. 2 Corinthians 3:7-9
8. Acts 15:28
9. Psalms 139, Romans 8:38-39, Isaiah 41:4, 46:10, Revelation 1:8, 22:13
10. Ps 37:23
11. Matthew 15:3, 6, Mark 7:8-9, 13, Col 2:8
12. Matthew 28:18-20, Luke 10:19, Romans 5:17, Ephesians 1:20-23, 2:5-6
13. Psalm 8, Genesis 1:27-28, 2:19, Psalm 115:16
14. Acts 16:6-7

Chapter 5
Here's Why You Can

1. 1 Corinthians 6:20, Gal 2:20
2. John 17
3. 1 Corinthians 2:12,16
4. Genesis 2:6,9,11,12
5. Genesis 3:8
6. Genesis 3:17-19
7. Matthew 25:34, Ephesians 1:4, John 17:5, 24, 1 Peter 1:20, Acts 2:23-24
8. Isaiah 53:5, Hebrews 4:16, 9:23, Romans 4:25
9. Colossians 2:14
10. Romans 10:9-10

11. Zechariah 9:12
12. John 1:12, Revelation 21:9
13. John 17:1, Matthew 26:53, John 3:35, 20:17, Luke 11:2-4
14. John 1:12, Hebrews 4:16, Romans 8:15, Galatians 4:6-7
15. Philippians 2:13
16. Romans 12:1-2, 2 Corinthians 5:17-18, Philemon 6
17. Ephesians 3:20, Romans 8:11
18. I Corinthians 2:12, Matthew 7:7-8
19. 2 Corinthians 5:17-18

Chapter 6
Free To Dream

1. Matthew 19:4-9
2. Matthew 22:23-33, Luke 20:27-40
3. Matthew 19:4-6
4. Genesis 5:2
5. Genesis 2
6. Genesis 1:26,28
7. 2 Peter 3:7,10, Matthew 24:35
8. Revelation 21:1
9. Revelation 20:6, 3:21, 22:5, Daniel 7:18, 27, Ephesians 2:7
10. 2 Corinthians 5:17-18
11. John 1:12
12. Ephesians 5:22-32
13. 1 Corinthians 7:2, 5
14. Philippians 4:8

15. Genesis 1 - 2
16. 2 Corinthians 5:17-18, 1 Corinthians 2:16
17. John 14:30
18. Romans 12:2

Chapter 7
Intentionally Unique

1. Genesis 1:26-28, Psalm 8, 115:16, Romans 1:19-20, 5:17
2. Romans 1:18-32
3. Matthew 22:37-38
4. Galatians 3:24
5. 1 John 4:19
6. Matthew 20:28
7. John 3:16
8. Genesis 1
9. Psalm 147:4, Isaiah 40:26

Chapter 8
What You Never Knew About Christopher Columbus

1. Americas God and Country, Copyright © 1996, 1994 by William J. Federer
2. John 16:33

Chapter 10
The City Lights and the Country Stars

1. Ps 147:4, Is 40:26

Chapter 11
The Beginning

1. John 10:1-18

2. Isaiah 54:17

Receiving Jesus as Your Lord

Choosing to make Jesus your Lord and Savior is the single most important decision you will ever make.

If you have never been saved and would like to be, if you're saved but have walked away from your life with the Lord, or you're not sure if you're saved and you want to be sure, and you want to receive all that He has done for you, simply believe and receive.

The Word of God says that *"if you believe in your heart that God raised Jesus from the dead, and you confess with your mouth that Jesus is Lord, you will be saved."* And again, *"All who call on the Name of the Lord will be saved."*

Rom 10:9-10, 13

It's easy. Just say this prayer, from your heart, out loud:

Jesus, I believe in my heart that God raised You from the dead, and I confess with my mouth that you are my Lord and Savior. By faith in Your Word, I receive salvation now. Thank You for saving me!

Now that you're born again, you are a brand-new you! The moment you received Jesus as Lord, God's Word was fulfilled in your spirit. Now begins the exiting journey of discovering all that belongs to you now that you belong to Jesus!

Tell someone. Let them rejoice with you. Give them the opportunity to take that same step. Find a place where you can meet other believers who will help you grow and learn more about this new life you now have.

Receive the Holy Spirit

Your loving Heavenly Father wants to give you – His child – supernatural power, His power, to live this new life you are now beginning.

Before He left, Jesus told His disciples, *"Wait for what the Father has promised which you heard of from Me,"* and, *"You will be baptized with the Holy Spirit not many days from now,"* and again, *"You will receive power when the Holy Spirit has come upon you."*   Acts 1:4, 5, 8

And His Word says that *"when they were all filled with the Holy Spirit they began to speak with other tongues as the Spirit was giving them the ability to speak out,"* and in another place, *"the Holy Spirit came upon them and they began speaking with tongues and prophesying."*   Acts 2:4, 19:6

He's made it so easy. All you have to do is ask, believe, and receive.

"For everyone that asks, receives; and he who seeks, finds; and to him who knocks, it shall be opened...how much more will your Heavenly Father give the Holy Spirit to those that ask Him?"   Luke 11:10-13

"He will baptize you with the Holy Spirit and fire."   Matthew 3:11

Pray this simple prayer:

Lord, I want Your power in my life. I want everything You purchased for me on the cross. Please baptize me with the Holy Spirit. Fill me. By faith, I receive it now. Thank you! Holy Spirit You are welcome in my life.

Congratulations! Now you are filled with God's power. Some words you don't know will begin to rise up in your spirit. Go ahead and speak them out loud. It will sound funny and feel strange at first, but go ahead anyway. You will find that it will soon become more natural to you than speaking in your native language.

So why pray in tongues? In Romans 8 we read, *"In the same way the Spirit also helps our weakness; for we do not know how to pray as we should, but the Spirit Himself intercedes for us with groanings too deep for words; and He who searches the hearts knows what the mind of the Spirit is, because He intercedes for the saints according to the will of God."*

And again, in Jude 1:20 it says, *"but you, beloved, building yourselves up on your most holy faith, praying in the Holy Spirit."*

And in Ephesians 6:18 it says, *"With all prayer and petition pray at all times in the Spirit, and with this in view, be on the alert with all perseverance and petition for all the saints."*

In his letter to the Corinthians, Paul said, *"I thank God I speak in tongues more than you all;"* and look at all he came up against and all he accomplished anyway.

All of God's promises are "yes" in Jesus, but we can't, with our natural knowledge, know all the things that we need to pray about in order to bring those promises to pass in the earth.

The Word "helps" in Rom 8:26 means "takes hold with another who is laboring." It's like when we're trying to move a piece of furniture. It's too big for one alone, but when someone takes hold of the other end, it can be easily moved. Having already received the promises, the Holy Spirit takes hold together with us and, working as a team, intercedes for us to bring the Father's will – the promises – into manifestation in the earth. We don't have to figure out what needs to be done or how to get those things done. He already knows. Instead we join together with

Him and go forward with His knowledge and power.

We don't have to be perfect and know everything. He's there for us, with us forever.

So then why pray in tongues?

- We don't know how to pray as we should
- We build ourselves up, strengthen ourselves, in our faith.
- The Lord urges us to pray at all times in the Spirit.

As you do, you are releasing God's power from within and speaking mysteries to God.

You will be praying things your mind doesn't even know about, for people you may not even know. You will be praying about issues in your own life you are not aware exist or need to be dealt with. You will be praying beyond your own ability and understanding. You can do this whenever you like. You will be praying God's perfect will in any situation.

See 1 Cor 14:2, 14, Jude 1:20, Rom 8:26-27

Jesus said, *"He who believes in Me, as the Scripture said, 'From his innermost being will flow rivers of living water.'"*   John 7:38

In the book of Jeremiah God describes Himself as the fountain of living waters, and in the book of Ezekiel we find a description of a river bringing life wherever it flows. Revelation 22:1–2 talks about the river of life that flows from the throne of God and of the Lamb, and Ezekiel 47:12 talks about that same river. When we speak in tongues as the Spirit gives us the words to speak, we are speaking things, not according to our own natural understanding, but according to the heart and mind of God. The rivers of living water that Jesus told us will flow from our innermost being are the same waters that are flowing from God's throne and His throne! Isn't that amazing?

The Bible tells us to earnestly desire spiritual gifts, but especially that you may prophesy. The gifts of the Spirit are given to help everyone, and are listed in 1 Corinthians, chapter 12. They are:

Words of wisdom

Words of knowledge

Gift of faith

Gifts of healing

Working of miracles

Discerning of spirits

Tongues

Interpretation of tongues

Prophecy

It is the Lord's desire that we earnestly desire these gifts to operate in our lives. As we do, we will not only grow spiritually ourselves and see amazing transformations in our own lives, but we will be a vessel for the Lord to use to help others.

It doesn't matter whether or not you felt anything when you received Jesus as your Lord or prayed to receive His Spirit. The Word of God promises that you did.

"And all things you ask in prayer, believing, you shall receive."   Matthew 21:22

God's Word is the final authority. His Word set the worlds in space and the stars in the heavens. His Word causes the sun to rise every morning. None of us sit around at 3 o'clock in the morning and worry about whether or not the sun is going to come up. We know it will, there's never a doubt about it, and we make plans accordingly. Be confident. Be assured. His Word, all His promises, are just as sure for you!

Rejoice! Thank Him. You have just begun the most wonderful journey of your life!

We would like to hear from you

If you prayed to receive Jesus as your Savior, or prayed to receive the Holy Spirit, or you have a testimony to share after reading this book, please contact us and let us know. We want to rejoice with you and help you understand more fully what has taken place in you and in your life.

DA@DestinyAlignment.com

About the Author

A master trained, certified Christian Life Coach, Cindy's primary passion is to see God's people live the life Jesus died to give them, to fulfill their destiny, to know how special they are and how much they are loved.

As the founder of Destiny Alignment, Cindy is dedicated to the belief that everyone is born with a destiny and uniquely equipped by God to fulfill that destiny, and joins in celebrating each person's individual greatness.

Many years ago she grew in the knowing that there was so much more to God than what she was hearing, seeing, and experiencing. She abandoned man's opinions and submitted to the Father and asked Him to teach her His Word, His ways, and who He was. She shares what she has learned in the Father's presence and watching the Holy Spirit at work throughout the earth.

The scriptures the Lord gave her to guide her life are:

"He must increase and I must decrease."

John 3:30

"If anyone is willing to do His will, he will know of the teaching, whether it is of God or whether I speak from Myself."   John 7:17

"Whatever He says to you, do it."   John 2:5

At the Lord's instruction, prophet Kim Clement was her mentor for more than 20 years. Cindy completed, with honors, three courses offered by the School of the Prophet taught by Kim – Prophetic Perceptions, Prophetic Revelations, and Prophetic Destiny.

In addition to a career in medicine, her background includes 15 years in ministry, 15 years as a dance instructor, and art, music, fitness and nutrition.

Born in Buffalo, New York and raised in Colorado, she continues to reside with her family in Colorado.

The A B Cs of Destiny Alignment

It's never too late

to Achieve

to Become

to Change

Because the Cross changed everything!

Vision: Our passion is for every one of God's people be transformed by renewing their minds so they can live freely in the fullness Jesus died to provide for them, and to know and live out the destiny that is waiting to be revealed to them.

Destiny Alignment –
Be all Jesus died for you to be

Destiny Alignment –
Because you have a destiny to
fulfill

Destiny Alignment –
Because it's time to take your
mountain

DestinyAlignment.com

**Coaching, Consulting, Art and Design
Services**

Destiny
ALIGNMENT
Coaching Consulting Art Design

www.DestinyAlignment.com

www.ingramcontent.com/pod-product-compliance
Lightning Source LLC
LaVergne TN
LVHW051503080426
835509LV00017B/1901